Editor
Heather Douglas

Editor in Chief
Ina Massler Levin, M.A.

Creative Director
Karen J. Goldfluss, M.S. Ed.

Illustrator
Clint McKnight

Cover Artist
Tony Carillo

Art Coordinator
Renée Mc Elwee

Imaging
James Edward Grace
Leonard P. Swierski

Publisher
Mary D. Smith, M.S. Ed.

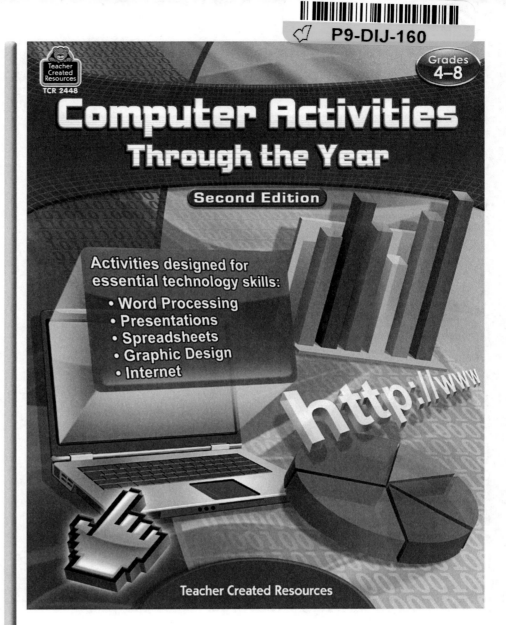

Grades 4–8

Computer Activities Through the Year

Second Edition

Activities designed for essential technology skills:
- Word Processing
- Presentations
- Spreadsheets
- Graphic Design
- Internet

http://www

Teacher Created Resources

TCR 2448

Author
Susan L. Gimotty, M.A.

Teacher Created Resources
12621 Western Avenue
Garden Grove, CA 92841
www.teachercreated.com
ISBN: 978-1-57690-448-0

©1999 Teacher Created Resources
Second edition published 2011
Reprinted, 2017
Made in U.S.A.

Teacher Created Resources

Table of Contents

Introduction. 4

Word Processing

Poems and More Poems. 5

In Charge of the World 10

I Am Thankful For. 12

Holiday Memories 14

Writing Prompts 16

Celebrating Presidents' Day 18

Showing Off Student Work 20

Snap That Picture! 24

Acrostic Poem 26

Letter Writing 30

Spreadsheet Skills

Creating a Word Search 33

Making a Bar Graph. 36

Comparative Bar Graph. 38

Making a Double Bar Graph 40

Pie, Bar, and Line Graphs. 42

Using Formulas on a Spreadsheet 44

Pictures on a Bar Graph 46

More Pie (Charts), Please 48

Input Internet Information. 50

Internet Skills

Research Report 52

Search Engines 54

Virtual Tour. 57

Determining Distance. 60

Map It! 63

Worldwide Weather 66

Finding and Using Clip Art. 69

Finding Information on the Net 71

Insects on the Internet. 73

Animals on the Internet 75

Computing Cost 77

Table of Contents *(cont.)*

Researching History 1 79
Researching History 2 81
Visiting National Parks 83
Finding Pictures 86
Top News Stories 88
White House Scavenger Hunt 91
Fact or Fiction? 96
The Planets 98

Presentations
All About Me 100
PowerPoint® Projects 102

Graphic Design
Designing Travel Brochures 105
Flow Charts 108
Creating Bookmarks 111
Scientific Illustration 114
Creating Cards 116
Making Flags 118
Coupon Gifts 120
Word Art 122
Door Hangers 124
Illustrating Quotes 126
Borders and Lines 128
Attractive Advertisements 130
Timelines 132
Making Projects Look Professional 134
The Food Guide 136
Creating a Cookbook 138
Making a Menu 140

Appendix
Software Descriptions 143

Links to websites
updated regularly at

http://www.teachercreated.com/url-updates/2448-2

Introduction

Technology is a critical element in most jobs and careers, necessary to becoming part of today's work force. Students are expected to have a considerable knowledge base of the necessary skills. *Computer Activities Through the Year, 2nd Edition*, offers instructions for projects that build students' skills using today's most common programs and applications. It also contains lessons that give students the opportunity to navigate and explore the Internet.

The 21st century has seen an explosion in information and technology. Google's CEO, Eric Schmidt, put it this way: "Every two days we create as much information as we did from the dawn of time until 2003." In order to keep up with the hyper-speed in which we are moving into the future, *Computer Activities Through the Year, 2nd Edition*, has been revised to accommodate the ever-changing domain of technology.

This book was written with the wide range of student ability levels in mind. The lessons can be easily tailored to ELL students and can challenge tech-savvy digital natives. The lessons effectively incorporate technology into activities that cover the required curriculum, enabling the teacher to not only enhance the subject area but also cover it more in depth.

The book is divided into five sections: Word Processing, Spreadsheet Skills, Internet Skills, Presentations, and Graphic Design. Each section covers skills that are necessary in today's technology-driven environment. Students will complete activities such as formatting documents, comparing data on a spreadsheet, using search engines to navigate the Internet, and creating visually appealing presentations.

Use this book to let your students explore new computer skills and enhance existing ones. This book is designed for use with any computer system, although the lessons often require specific types of software. Each lesson has an Application Needed section that offers suggestions for specific software. (See the Appendix for more detailed descriptions of the software used.) Make sure when having students access the Internet, to put an acceptable use policy for Internet safety in place based on your school and district guidelines.

Enjoy watching your students learn and grow in their computer skills as they complete the activities throughout the year.

Poems and More Poems

Objectives:

- Understanding different types of poetry such as haiku, tanka, cinquain, and limerick
- Counting syllables in words correctly
- Typing extemporaneously
- Centering and underlining titles
- Accessing clip art from a CD-ROM
- Spell-checking documents

Application Needed:

Use a word-processing application (program) such as *Microsoft Word*® or *Corel WordPerfect*®. Have clip art accessible from a CD-ROM or the Internet.

Instructions:

1. Discuss with students different types of poetry, such as the haiku, tanka, cinquain, and limerick. Explain to students about counting syllables. Show them the example of each type of format on the next few pages. (The students can pick one poem to do or make a poetry booklet containing many forms of poetry.)

2. Students will choose their poem formats and begin typing titles. Demonstrate how to center and underline the title.

3. Students will begin typing the bodies of their poems extemporaneously, keeping in mind the syllable and line structure.

4. Put students in pairs to check one another's poems for content and form.

5. Students can then find appropriate pictures to illustrate their poems from a CD-ROM or the Internet.

6. Each student's work should be spell-checked and printed.

Extension Ideas:

Poetry books make nice gifts for a parent or grandparent. Consider having each student choose a theme for his or her poetry book. Students may want to post some of their best poetry on the Internet or on the school Web site. Consider pairing your students with younger students to teach the basics of how to write a poem.

Poems and More Poems *(cont.)*

Haiku Poem

<u>Bustling Bees</u>

The bees are busy

Finding petals to land on

Quiet springtime hum

Haiku Format

Haiku is a form of unrhymed poetry that had its beginning in Japan. Haiku poetry usually describes something about nature or the seasons. Each poem is three lines and the number of syllables in each line follows this pattern:

Line 1: five syllables

Line 2: seven syllables

Line 3: five syllables

Poems and More Poems (cont.)

Tanka Poem

Icicles on the Trees

The pine trees are tall

Covered with snowflakes and ice

Swaying in the wind

Soon it will all sadly melt

But it was a sight to see

Tanka Format

According to Asian tradition, if someone writes you a haiku poem, you are to write a tanka poem in return to them. It is a way of saying thank you. The tanka poem does not have to be on the same subject. A tanka is five lines long and the number of syllables in each line follows this pattern:

Line 1: five syllables

Line 2: seven syllables

Line 3: five syllables

Line 4: seven syllables

Line 5: seven syllables

Poems and More Poems (cont.)

Cinquain Poem

Flowers

Flowers

Colorful, delicate

Filled with fragrance

Lulling me into dreams

Blossoms

Cinquain Format

A cinquain is a simple, five-line verse that follows this form:

Line 1: one noun (the subject of the poem)

Line 2: two adjectives (words that describe the subject of the poem)

Line 3: three-word phrase (telling an action of the subject)

Line 4: four words (expressing a feeling about the subject)

Line 5: another noun describing the subject (a synonym)

Poems and More Poems *(cont.)*

Limerick Poem

The Boy From Delray

There once was a boy from Delray,

Who was light as a feather they say.

The wind came along,

And blew very strong,

And carried the poor boy away.

Limerick Format

A limerick is a short, silly poem. Most limericks are five lines long following these rules:

Lines 1, 2, and 5 rhyme.

Lines 1, 2 and 5 have eight, nine, or ten beats.

Lines 3 and 4 rhyme.

Lines 3 and 4 have either five, six, or seven beats.

In Charge of the World

Objectives:

- Using the Tab key
- Typing extemporaneously
- Spell-checking a document
- Learning how to word process in poetry format

Application Needed:

Use basic word-processing application such as *Microsoft Word®* or *Corel WordPerfect®*.
It would be helpful to have clip art available too.

Instructions:

1. There is a popular poem by Judith Viorst entitled "If I Were In Charge of the World." Find this poem online and read it to the class. Discuss what it would be like to be in charge of the world. Ask the students about things they would like to do if they were in charge of the world.

2. Students will be writing their own poems entitled "If I Were In Charge of the World." You may want to have younger students brainstorm on a piece of paper what they would do if they were in charge of the world. Older students should be able to type extemporaneously on the computer.

3. Demonstrate how to put their work in poetry format. Explain to students the meaning of the Tab key and show them how to use it. Stress to students that the Tab key should be used instead of the Space Bar key. Although a document may appear aligned on the monitor, when a person uses the Space Bar key to indent, often times the document will not print aligned.

4. Once students are finished typing, have them spell check their poems.

5. Finally, they need to proof and print their work.

Extension Ideas:

Students are infatuated with the idea of being in charge. A teacher could change the title to ask students what they would do if they were in charge of the entire school. If you are studying a particular country, such as Argentina, change the title to "If I Were In Charge of Argentina." There are many other poems that are ideal for a springboard, particularly some of Shel Silverstein's work.

In Charge of the World *(cont.)*

If I Were In Charge of the World

If I were in charge of the world

I'd make weekends longer,

Doctor appointments shorter, and

Brussel sprouts obsolete.

If I were in charge of the world

People would be more friendly,

School bus drivers would let us sing, and

Parents would have a bedtime!

If I were in charge of the world

All pets would have owners,

People would think twice before they smoke,

Moms would have help around the house, and

Someone would find the cure for cancer.

If I were in charge of the world

Trash would be in garbage cans, and

Popcorn would be free at the movies.

This world would be a much better place

If I were in charge of the world.

I Am Thankful For...

Objectives:

- Perfecting typing skills
- Moving text to center page in a word-processing application
- Changing the color or font of text in a word-processing application
- Multitasking (using more than one program at the same time)
- Copying and pasting from the clipboard

Application Needed:

Use a word-processing application such as *Microsoft Word*® or *Corel WordPerfect*®. You will also need clip art available, preferably from another application so students have the opportunity to use more than one program at the same time.

Instructions:

1. Using a piece of scrap paper, students should write the word THANKSGIVING one letter at a time, going down.
2. Students should think of things for which they are thankful, keeping in mind that the first letter of each line needs to correspond with a letter from the word THANKSGIVING. See the example on the next page.
3. Have students type their rough drafts, keeping them left justified (don't center or tab text).
4. Highlight the entire text once it is all typed. Using the header ruler, move the text over to the middle. The word THANKSGIVING should still be in a straight line going down.
5. Highlight only the "T" of the first line. Change the color of the "T".
6. Continue this process until all of the first letters are the same color. Change the color of the title, too. Keep the remaining text black.
7. Keeping the word-processing application open, go into the clip-art application, either on the hard drive or on a CD-ROM. If necessary, resize the window in order to launch the second application.
8. Students should locate clip art that would look appropriate and copy it to the clipboard. (Edit, Copy)
9. Students should then go back into their word-processing document and paste their pictures. (Edit, Paste)
10. Move or resize the picture if necessary.

Extension Ideas:

Ideas that would work nicely would be to use the students' name or the name of a famous person like George Washington. Students could use phrases that describe themselves or the famous person.

I Am Thankful For... *(cont.)*

The birds that sing

Having loving parents

Ability to play sports

Nice brother

Keeping good grades

Singing in the choir

Good health

Ice cream

Varsity soccer

Incredible friends

Nature

Great school

Holiday Memories

Objectives:

- Perfecting typing skills
- Centering text
- Using spell-check
- Adding clip art to a word-processing document
- Copying and pasting from the clipboard
- Multitasking (using more than one program at the same time)

Application Needed:

Use a word-processing application such as *Microsoft Word*® or *Corel WordPerfect*®. You will also need clip art available, preferably from another application so students have the opportunity to use more than one application at the same time.

Instructions:

1. Have students think of a fond memory that relates to the holiday season. Emphasize that the memory should be specific. See the example on the next page.

2. Depending on the students' ages and typing abilities, you may want them to write a quick rough draft. Otherwise, have them type extemporaneously.

3. Students should center text.

4. After all typing is finished, students should change the font style and size of the text to fill up approximately half a page and then spell-check the document.

5. Keeping the word-processing application open, go into the clip art application, either on the hard drive or on a CD-ROM. If necessary, resize the window in order to launch the second application.

6. Students should locate clip art that would look appropriate on the letter and copy it to the clipboard. (Edit, Copy)

7. Open the word-processing document again and paste the picture. (Edit, Paste)

8. Move or resize the picture if necessary.

Extension Ideas:

This lesson is primarily designed to teach multitasking. Any topic would work with this lesson, provided you have suitable clip art available. Seasonal projects are always fun to do, and this particular one makes a lovely gift to a parent. Another suggestion would be to use this idea for state reports. Students could write 2–3 paragraphs of information and then paste their states at the bottom. Compile all reports and make a class book.

Holiday Memories *(cont.)*

Dear Mom and Dad,

One holiday memory that I will never forget is the time our family had a slumber party on Christmas Eve by our Christmas tree. Remember, we had hot chocolate and cookies right before we went to sleep. We left some out for Santa, too! I'm almost sure that I heard reindeer hooves on our roof that night. What a great memory, Mom and Dad. Thank you!

Love,
Taylor

Writing Prompts

Objectives:

- Typing extemporaneously
- Spell-checking a document accurately
- Changing font styles and sizes
- Understanding correct spacing in word processing, especially with punctuation

Application Needed:

Students will need a basic word-processing application such as *Microsoft Word*® or *Corel WordPerfect*®.

Instructions:

1. Students will read the six story starters on the next page and choose one to use.

2. Decide how the students should begin their stories. Students could retype the writing prompt. Another option would be for students to open up a document containing all six prompts and then delete all the prompts except for the one they want. Students would then begin typing, remembering to save this document with a new name.

3. Students will type the rest of their responses extemporaneously. Emphasize that the stories have a beginning, middle, and ending.

4. Explain to students about spacing. One space goes in between words and after commas; two spaces go after all end marks. (Another school of thought cites that only one space is needed after end marks. Decide which is best for your school.)

5. Students should spell check their documents. Explain that they must be cautious with spell-check…It is not a fix all.

6. Consider putting students in pairs for proofreading. Then have them print their stories.

7. Make sure students save their work for future editing, especially if you desire to make this a complete writing project including a rough draft and a final draft.

Extension Ideas:

Writing prompts are appropriate for any holiday, season, or subject matter. A teacher could make a book of writing prompts to be used at the computer when students finish their work. For upper-level students, the teacher could also make their prompts more like essay questions, such as, "What troubles did Columbus encounter before he discovered America?" Students also like to make their own writing prompts for classmates or to use themselves.

Writing Prompts *(cont.)*

Narrative Prompts

I could tell that it was going to be one of those days. Nothing seemed to go right all day. I was mindlessly sitting at my desk when all of a sudden, the classroom door swung open and there appeared . . .

There were two feet of snow on the ground with another foot expected to fall by the end of day. We could hardly believe our eyes! Our little city, which barely got six inches of snow all winter, was in the middle of a blizzard.

Holiday Prompts

Everyone knew that Santa was only a myth, but our views began to change after last Christmas Eve. We were all sitting around the tree sharing stories of the past when we heard a rustling in the chimney. We assumed it was birds, so we continued on with our stories. Then out of the clear night sky . . .

Going on an Easter egg hunt was one of my favorite pastimes. My parents put one quarter in each egg and hid at least 25 of them around the house. This Easter was a little different because no one could find the hidden eggs, even my parents. We decided . . .

Examples of Essay Questions

If Martin Luther King Jr. were alive today, how do you think he would feel about the race relations at our school?

It takes many qualities to become the president of the United States. Name two or three qualities which you feel are most important to being a successful president and why.

Celebrating Presidents' Day

Objectives:

- Perfecting typing skills
- Typing extemporaneously
- Using spell-check
- Adding clip art to a word processing document
- Multitasking

Application Needed:

Use a word-processing application such as *Microsoft Word®* or *Corel WordPerfect®*. You will also need clip art available, preferably from another application so students have the opportunity to use more than one application at the same time.

Instructions:

1. Have students choose a president in honor of Presidents' Day. (They may want to consider clip art availability when choosing a president.)

2. Depending on the students' age and typing ability, you may want them to write a quick rough draft. Otherwise, have them type extemporaneously, starting with the following sentence: I think Abraham Lincoln (or enter your president's name) would be proud of America for a variety of reasons.

3. Students should indent each paragraph by using the Tab key.

4. After all typing is finished, students should change the font style and size of the text to fill up approximately half a page.

5. Spell-check document.

6. Keeping the word-processing application open, go into your clip-art application, either on the hard drive or on a CD-ROM. If necessary, resize the window in order to launch the second application.

7. Students should locate clip art that would look appropriate and copy it to the clipboard. (Edit, Copy)

8. Go back to the word-processing document and paste the picture. (Edit, Paste)

9. Move or resize the picture if necessary.

Extension:

Any topic would work with this lesson, provided you have suitable clip art available. Students could also learn to use the scanner, and then there would be many options.

Celebrating Presidents' Day *(cont.)*

I think George Washington would be proud of America today for a variety of reasons. Being quite the soldier himself, he would be very impressed with our armed forces. He would be very proud of all the Americans who have given their lives throughout the years to protect our country. It would please Washington to see all the advancements we've made in modern medicine, too. Many of his men died due to simple causes that could have been easily cured today.

Washington would probably be surprised to see all of America's modern inventions such as automobiles, telephones, and computers. He would probably be shocked at how wasteful we are with these modern technologies.

I think Washington would be delighted that we are still one nation in spite of our vast growth. He would be thrilled to take a tour of Washington, DC to see the many monuments, memorials, and the White House.

Showing Off Student Work

Objectives:

- Perfecting typing skills
- Typing extemporaneously
- Setting margins
- Using spell-check

Application Needed:

Use a word-processing application such as *Microsoft Word*® or *Corel WordPerfect*®. It would be preferable to use the word-processing application that you use most often so students can be familiar with the items on the toolbar. You will also need to buy stationery that can be fed through the printer.

Instructions:

1. Students should set the margins depending on the stationery. Most of the time, you can set the margins by clicking File, Page Setup. You may need to consult your manual. You will need to experiment with the margins to get the exact setting for your particular stationery.

2. Depending on the students' age and typing ability, you may want them to write a quick rough draft. Otherwise, have them type extemporaneously a poem or short story related to the theme of the stationery.

3. If students are putting text in paragraph form, then they should indent each paragraph by using the Tab key.

4. After all typing is finished, students should change the font style and size of the text to fill the page.

5. Spell-check the document.

6. It is wise to print stories on plain white paper first, just to make sure there are no errors. Spell-check does not catch every mistake. Later, reprint on the special stationery.

Extension Ideas:

For this lesson, extension ideas are contingent on the type of stationery you are able to buy. Computer stores, office-supply stores, and catalogs are good places to look for fancy stationery. Letters to Mom or Dad are always a hit, especially when you mail them. Parents may want to frame seasonal poetry that is printed on nice stationery.

Showing Off Student Work (cont.)

Winter is...
Drinking hot chocolate by the fire
Seeing Christmas lights
Throwing snowballs
Dad reading the Christmas story to us
Ice skating at our pond
Staying home from school on snow days
Working puzzles with Mom and Dad
Wearing thick, cable sweaters
Being in the holiday pageant
Spending time with relatives
Going caroling in the neighborhood
Dreaming that spring would come soon

Showing Off Student Work *(cont.)*

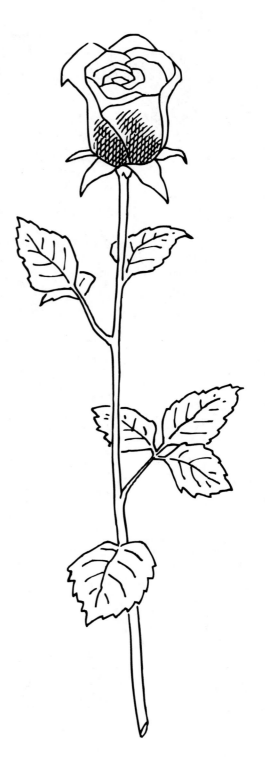

May 13

Dear Mom,

I want to wish you a special Mother's Day. You are one terrific mom! My life would be very boring without you. I'm lucky to have you as my mom.

I really appreciate all of the nice things you do for me. You always take me to soccer on Thursdays, even though I know some days that you are tired. You also do fun things with me. Remember when we were making a cake for my last birthday and we got frosting on the ceiling? What a memory that was!

You are also a great cook! My favorite meal you make is spaghetti and garlic bread. Don't you ever get tired of cleaning up after all of us? I'm sorry we make such a mess. Thank you for going to the pool with us on Saturdays, too.

Mom, you are great! I hope that you will have a wonderful Mother's Day. You deserve it!

I love you,

Madison

Showing Off Student Work *(cont.)*

It's a Wonderful Time of Year

Delicate flowers emerging

From their quiet state.

Animals scurrying around looking

For their daily food supply.

Trees waking up

From a long winter's sleep.

Chirping birds pleased

To make a joyful noise.

Lighthearted people eager

For spring to be near.

It is indeed

A wonderful time of year!

Snap That Picture!

Objectives:

- Using a digital camera
- Cropping pictures on the computer
- Pasting digital pictures into a document
- Spell checking a document accurately

Application Needed:

Students will need a digital camera, software for the digital camera, and a word-processing application such as *Microsoft Word®* or *Corel WordPerfect®*.

Instructions:

1. Students will create a project, such as a totem pole or Egyptian pyramid.
2. The teacher will take a picture with the digital camera of each student holding his or her project.
3. Depending on the skill level and class time available, the teacher or students will access the pictures from the camera. Often times pictures will need cropping, which can be done in the digital camera software or in the drawing part of a word processing application such as *Microsoft Word®*.
4. Students will type a paragraph or two about their projects, including the method of construction, meaning of artwork, etc.
5. Students should spell-check their documents. Explain that they must be cautious with the spell-check, it is not a fix all.
6. Consider putting students in pairs for proofreading.
7. Have students add their pictures to the side or bottom of their documents and then print their work.

Extension Ideas:

The digital camera is a great resource at any school. Teachers can take the camera on a field trip and view the pictures later for class discussion. Teachers can take pictures of their students at the beginning of the year to use on folders, bulletin boards, or weekly newsletters. Students may want to take pictures of their artwork and compile an art portfolio. When students are working on a group project and everyone cannot take the final project home, take pictures of the project and distribute them to all members of the group.

Snap That Picture! *(cont.)*

My Totem Pole

My totem pole is in the shape of a polar bear. Polar bears are large creatures who lead rather solitary lives roaming for food. It is surprising, though, how fast polar bears can run when challenged by another animal. Polar bears enjoy the water and playful swimming.

I chose the polar bear because it is an animal similar to me. I am rather big for my age, at least that is what everyone tells me. I enjoy being by myself and love a good meal. People look at me and think that I cannot run very fast because of my size, but they are shocked to find out that I am quite a fast runner. Lastly, I enjoy the water. I go to the neighborhood pool on many summer days. I have been a member of the swim team for the past three years.

Acrostic Poem

Objectives:

- Typing extemporaneously
- Setting margins
- Formatting first letter to desired color and size
- Perfecting spell-checking skills
- Highlighting specified text

Application Needed:

Use a word processing application such as *Microsoft Word*® or *Corel WordPerfect*®. It would be preferable to use the word-processing application that you use most often so students can quickly become familiar with the items on the toolbar.

Instructions:

1. Students should type their title and center it. Have students use a font size somewhere between 18 and 24 point.

2. Depending on the students' age and typing ability, you may want them to write a quick rough draft. Otherwise, have them type an acrostic poem spelling EARTH DAY vertically. Each line should be a few words or a phrase.

3. Once students have finished typing their poems, have them spell-check their documents. Remember, spell-check does not catch every mistake!

4. Next, have the students highlight the first letter of each line (which spells EARTH DAY). With the first letter highlighted, change the font color, bold it, and increase the size. (Many programs change the font color, style, and size by going to Format, then Font.) Continue highlighting the first letter of each line until all letters are changed.

5. Have students add clip art pertinent to Earth Day by copying and pasting it from another application or the Internet. If time is of importance, you may want to preprint paper with a piece of Earth Day clip art at the bottom of each page.

6. Preview students' work prior to printing to make sure it fits on the page correctly. Then print.

Extension Ideas:

Acrostics are popular with students because they give some structure to poetry. One could do this with any holiday, curriculum subject, or use students' names. These poems also make terrific gifts for parents or grandparents. See the examples that follow.

Acrostic Poem *(cont.)*

Earth Day

Every day the ozone layer is threatened.

Always put trash in the garbage.

Reusing items will help save the Earth.

Trash goes in the garbage, not on the ground.

How often do you recycle?

Don't pollute; it is our Earth to share.

Are you conserving water?

You are Earth's most valuable resource.

Acrostic Poem *(cont.)*

Madison

Misses her dog, Brandy

Always likes pepperoni pizza

Does the dishes every other day

Is interested in drawing and painting

Sings in the church choir

Only has one brother named Scott

Never has had her ears pierced

Acrostic Poem (cont.)

Sharks

Some sharks are fierce predators,

Have a sleek, streamlined design.

A mother shark carries her babies inside her body,

Rarely kills people,

Keeps growing new teeth.

Some eat large prey such as sea turtles.

Letter Writing

Objectives:

- Understanding the basic format of a letter (both business and friendly)
- Indenting paragraphs (friendly letter)
- Using toolbar rules to move text (friendly letter)
- Spell-checking a document

Application Needed:

A basic word processing application, such as *Microsoft Word*®, or *Corel WordPerfect*® will work well for this project.

Instructions:

1. The teacher should assign a particular letter format for students, either a friendly letter or business letter. For business letter, students will need to be supplied with the correct address of the business or organization.

2. Students will follow the format on page 32 for a business letter. Students should include the date, name and address of recipient, greeting, body of letter, and salutation. All text will be justified to the left with no indents for paragraphs.

3. A friendly letter has a different format, like the sample on the next page. Paragraphs are indented (press tab one time). The date and the closing are indented over to the 2 1/2 or 3 inch mark on the toolbar ruler. Students will need to be shown how to use the toolbar ruler effectively.

4. Once students have typed all of their information, they may need to enlarge or shrink the font size to fill the page comfortably.

5. Work should be proofed, spell-checked, and then printed.

Extension Ideas:

Letter writing reinforces many basic computer skills. The teacher may have each student bring in a business letter from home to discuss the correct format. (Make sure the letters do not contain confidential information.)

Students also enjoy writing friendly letters. Team up with another teacher in some other state or country and have pen pals for your students. Students could also write letters of appreciation to a loved one.

Also, discuss with students how to properly address an envelope.

Letter Writing *(cont.)*

November 15, 2012

Dear Dr. Harrison,

I would like to write to you a letter of appreciation thanking you for all of the wonderful things you have done for Southfield Middle School in the last two years. You have made a significant impact on our school in such a short time. The whole city was well aware of this when we won the Blue Ribbon Award last April.

I really enjoy seeing your smiling face in the morning as I am getting off the bus. I always know when you are sick or out of town because those are the only days I do not see you on the sidewalk. I also like how you have rearranged the lunch schedule. Prior to your coming, students were eating lunch very late in the afternoon, even as late as 1:45 PM. With your new system everyone is finished eating by 1:00 PM, and the students are very happy. I love it when you come to our Saturday 7th–8th grade basketball games. We all seem to play a little harder knowing you're watching.

I know you work long hours at Southfield Middle, but I want to tell you that it is worth it. You have made our school a finer place. I hope you stay for many more years.

Sincerely,

Steven Daniel

Letter Writing (cont.)

August 25, 2012

Mrs. Pauline Hawke
Bald Eagle Bed and Breakfast
1685 Main Street
Bangor, MN 04401

Dear Mrs. Hawke,

I understand that you are the manager of the Bald Eagle Bed & Breakfast. I am designing a trip for my 6th grade geography class project. We are assigned to visit three national parks and find accommodations at each. According to the Internet, your bed-and-breakfast is within a few miles of Acadia National Park. For my class project, I thought that I would like to stay at the Bald Eagle Bed & Breakfast. By the way, I thought your Internet website was very informative.

Could you please send me brochures showing your bed-and-breakfast and include room rates? Also, could you send me any information about Acadia National Park that you may have? Thank you very much. My address is 14321 Debbs Lane, Chesapeake, Virginia 23320.

Sincerely,

Brian Pole

Creating a Word Search

Objectives:

- Perfecting spreadsheet skills
- Changing column width of cells
- Copying and pasting from the clipboard
- Multitasking (using more than one program at the same time)

Application Needed:

Use an application that has spreadsheet capability, such as *Microsoft Excel*®. You will also need some type of clip art.

Instructions:

1. Have students write down 8–10 words that all pertain to the same subject but are not more than 10 letters long each.
2. Using a spreadsheet, have students section off a block.
3. Reduce column width of all cells in the block to 3.
4. Capitalize and center letters in each cell, one letter per cell.
5. First, students type in the words that are in their word banks. Challenge students to make words go diagonally and backwards, too.
6. Once all of the word-bank words are entered, students will fill in empty cells with other letters. To be more tricky, they shouldn't put just random letters in the empty cells. They can make words that are similar to their word bank lists but spelled differently or slightly incorrect.
7. Then they will highlight the block, and take off the gridlines if they wish.
8. Depending on which application you use, students may need to highlight the grid and import it into a graphic/clip art application.
9. Have students add a title, word bank, and pictures.
10. Proof the work and print.

Extension Ideas:

The best way to use this word search idea is to integrate it into the curriculum. This is a nice culminating project for any vocabulary or spelling unit. It could also be one of the requirements for the project booklet. Any topic would work, such as plants, seasons, presidents, marine life, or space.

Creating a Word Search (cont.)

C	A	L	I	F	O	R	N	I	A
R	G	H	O	S	T	T	O	W	N
C	O	W	B	O	Y	S	K	O	W
G	L	H	J	K	L	B	C	E	A
H	D	P	O	B	G	R	A	S	G
U	R	A	I	L	R	O	A	D	O
K	U	Y	R	E	G	B	E	R	N
L	S	M	I	N	E	R	S	I	S
D	H	P	C	A	R	I	B	O	U

Words to Find:

GOLD RUSH

COWBOYS

CALIFORNIA

MINERS

WAGONS

CARIBOU

RAILROAD

GHOST TOWN

Creating a Word Search (cont.)

D	H	S	W	L	A	D	T	L
R	O	T	E	I	R	O	R	A
M	N	E	P	T	U	N	E	S
U	A	T	R	L	S	P	S	H
S	T	R	L	O	U	R	H	U
R	E	H	S	T	K	T	P	T
A	M	O	O	N	R	N	O	T
T	C	M	H	A	M	C	B	L
S	A	T	E	L	L	I	T	E

Words to Find:

MOON

SHUTTLE

EARTH

NEPTUNE

SATELLITE

MARS

STARS

PLUTO

Making a Bar Graph

Objectives:

- Understanding the basics of a spreadsheet
- Making a horizontal bar graph
- Highlighting cells in a spreadsheet
- Changing colors of the bars in a bar graph
- Becoming familiar with spreadsheet terms such as *X-axis* and *Y-axis*.

Application Needed:

A spreadsheet application will be necessary for this project, such as *Microsoft Excel®*. Clip art should also be available.

Instructions:

1. Have students find all of the planets' average distances from the sun either in a book or from the Internet.

2. Students will open the spreadsheet and enter data similar to the diagram shown below. Students will graph all of the plants, not just the first five as shown here.

3. Once the data is entered, students should highlight all of the cells with information in them.

4. Students will then make a horizontal bar graph. The chart should include the name of each planet and its distance from the sun.

5. Explain the X-axis and Y-axis to students and tell them why it is so important to label the unit of distance, whether it is kilometers, miles, centimeters, etc.

6. Students can change the color and pattern of the bars.

7. Students should add an appropriate title and clip art, and then print their work.

Extension Ideas:

Graphing is an important skill for students to learn. Students could graph other things such as miles to the gallon on different cars, distances from school to each student's house, or free-throw percentages for NBA players.

	Distance (mi)
Mercury	36,000,000
Venus	67,000,000
Earth	93,000,000
Mars	141,000,000
Jupiter	483,000,000

Making a Bar Graph (cont.)

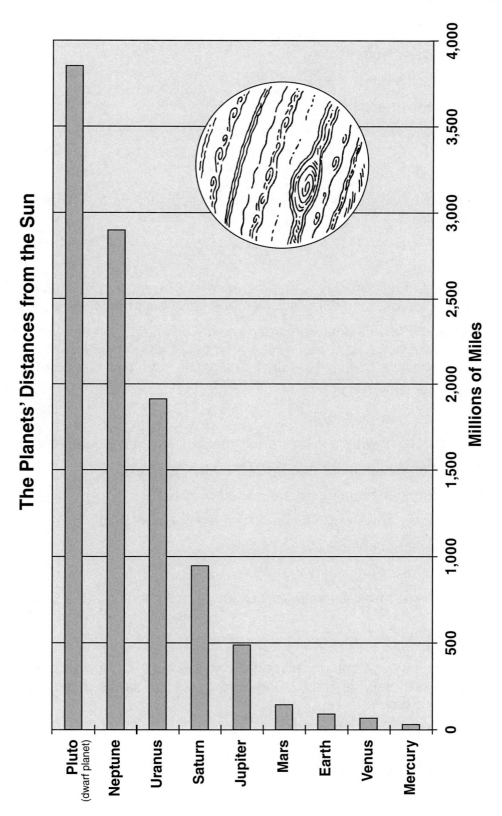

The Planets' Distances from the Sun

Millions of Miles

4,000
3,500
3,000
2,500
2,000
1,500
1,000
500
0

Pluto (dwarf planet)
Neptune
Uranus
Saturn
Jupiter
Mars
Earth
Venus
Mercury

Comparative Bar Graph

Objectives:

- Understanding a basic spreadsheet
- Learning terms such as *cell*, *X-axis*, and *Y-axis*
- Entering data into a spreadsheet
- Copying and pasting clip art from another application

Application Needed:

A spreadsheet application will be necessary for this project, such as *Microsoft Excel®*. Clip art should also be available.

Instructions:

1. Discuss spreadsheet terminology with the students. The basic terminology that you need to know is "cell," "X-axis," and "Y-axis." Demonstrate how to enter data into a cell.

2. Collect class data. Pick a student recorder to write down data on the whiteboard. Ask how many students have dogs, cats, etc. Get a total count for dogs. Next move on to a total count for cats. Continue this process until all animals have been recorded.

3. In cell A2, enter the word "DOGS."

4. In cell A3, enter the word "CATS."

5. Continue this process down the A column until all animals have been typed.

6. In cell B2, enter the total number of dogs owned by the class.

7. In cell B3, enter the total number of cats owned by the class.

8. Continue this process down until all numbers have been entered.

9. Use the data to create a comparative bar graph.

10. Add a chart title, X-axis title, and a Y-axis title.

11. Copy and paste clip art from another application to make it more attractive.

Extension Ideas:

Use different topics such as eye color or favorite subject in school. Add another dimension to your graph by doing a comparative graph. Show not only your class's data but also that of all of the other classes in your grade.

Comparative Bar Graph (cont.)

Comparing 3 Classes of Data

	A	B	C	D	E
1		CLASS 5A	CLASS 5B	CLASS 5C	
2	DOGS	10	12	5	
3	CATS	5	2	9	
4	BIRDS	1	1	2	
5	FISH	13	7	11	
6	LIZARDS	1	1	1	

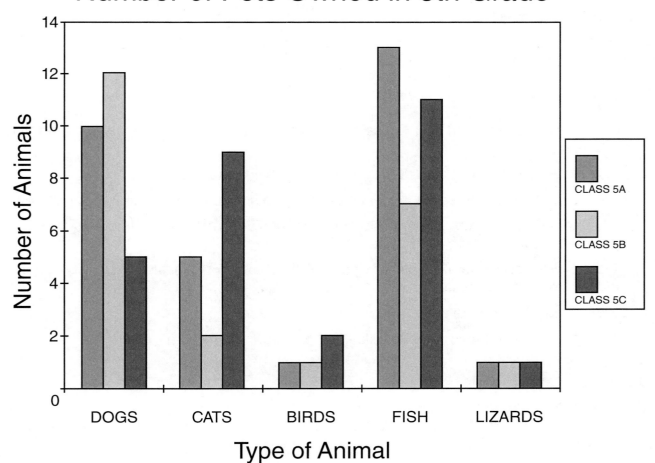

Number of Pets Owned in 5th Grade

Making a Double Bar Graph

Objectives:

- Understanding the basics of spreadsheets
- Making a double bar graph
- Highlighting cells in a spreadsheet
- Becoming familiar with spreadsheet terms such as *Y-axis* and *X-axis*.
- Changing colors of the bars in a bar graph

	Boys	Girls
Stuffing	12	8
Turkey	20	15
Mashed Potatoes	20	15
Green Beans	8	6
Cranberries	12	8
Ham	11	14
Pumpkin Pie	16	8

Application Needed:

A spreadsheet application will be necessary for this project, such as *Microsoft Excel*®. Clip art should also be available.

Instructions:

1. Have students brainstorm their top seven favorite foods at Thanksgiving. Write them on the board.
2. Have students vote for each food they like to eat on Thanksgiving.
3. Have students open the spreadsheet and enter data similar to the diagram shown above.
4. Once the data is entered, students should highlight all of the cells with information, including the words "Boys" and "Girls."
5. Students will then make a double-bar graph. The chart should include the name of each food and the number of students who like it (boys and girls).
6. Students can change the color and pattern of the bars.
7. Students should add an appropriate title and clip art and print their work.

Extension Ideas:

This idea will work with many topics, but especially with personal preferences such as favorite colors and favorite sports. This is a good project for the beginning of the year in order to get acquainted with your students and their interests.

Making a Double Bar Graph *(cont.)*

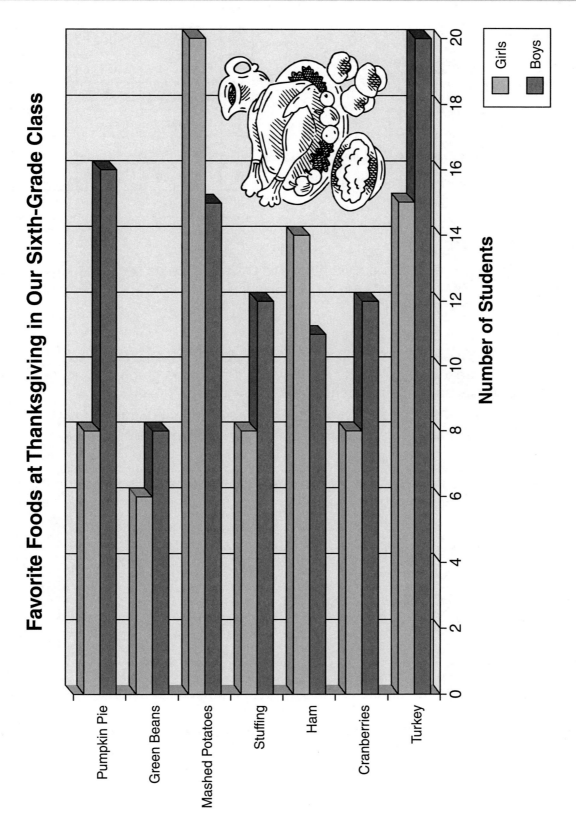

Pie, Bar, and Line Graphs

Objectives:

- Understanding a basic spreadsheet
- Learning terms such as a cell, X-axis, and Y-axis
- Entering data into a spreadsheet
- Understanding the pie, bar, and line graphs
- Copying and pasting clip art from another program

	A	B	C	D
1		CLASS 6A	CLASS 6B	
2	Colorado	6	2	
3	Texas	2	4	
4	Stayed Home	7	8	
5	Michigan	2	1	
6	Florida	3	4	

Application Needed:

A spreadsheet application will be necessary for this project, such as *Microsoft Excel®*. Clip art should also be available.

Instructions:

1. Discuss spreadsheet terminology with your students. The basic terminology they need to know is "cell," "X-axis," and "Y-axis." (If they are doing a pie graph, it is not necessary to discuss the X-axis and Y-axis.) Demonstrate how to enter data into a cell.
2. Collect class data. Pick a student recorder to write down data on the whiteboard. Get a total count for the entire class as to where they went on their holiday break.
3. In cell A2, enter the first destination.
4. In cell A3, enter the next destination. Continue this process down in the A column until all destinations have been typed.
5. In cell B2, enter the total number of students who went to destination #1.
6. Continue this process down until all numbers have been entered.
7. Use the data to create the graph.
8. Add a chart title, X-axis title, and Y-axis title.
9. Copy and paste clip art.

Extension Ideas:

Use different topics instead of holiday break, such as summer vacation or cities where students were born. Add another dimension to your graph by doing a comparative graph. (See the example on the next page.) You will need to enter your data into the spreadsheet slightly differently, as in the example above.

Pie, Bar, and Line Graphs *(cont.)*

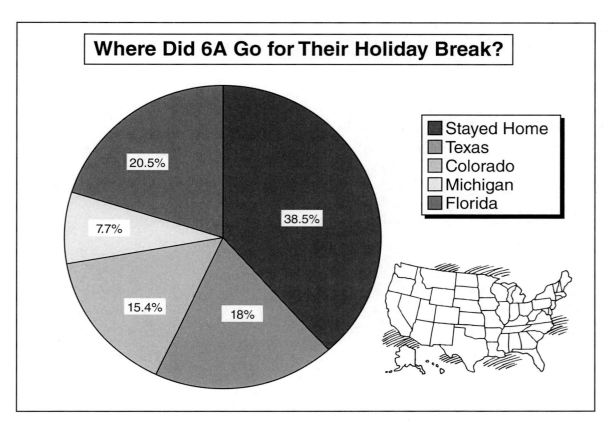

Where Did 6A Go for Their Holiday Break?

Legend:
- Stayed Home
- Texas
- Colorado
- Michigan
- Florida

38.5% · 18% · 15.4% · 7.7% · 20.5%

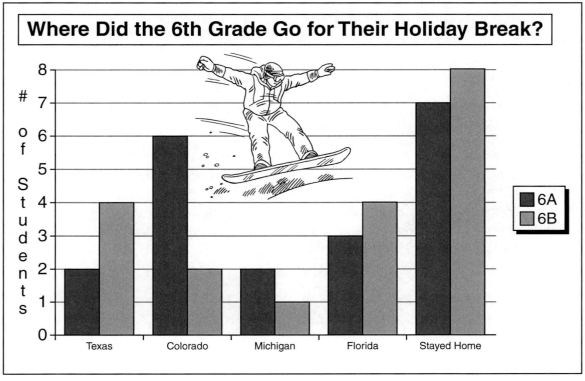

Where Did the 6th Grade Go for Their Holiday Break?

of Students

Texas · Colorado · Michigan · Florida · Stayed Home

Legend: 6A, 6B

Using Formulas on a Spreadsheet

Objectives:

- Understanding the basics of a spreadsheet, such as a cell, the name of each cell (A1 or C8), etc.
- Entering data into the cells on a spreadsheet
- Understanding formulas on a spreadsheet
- Entering the correct formulas on a spreadsheet starting with the equals sign

Application Needed:

Use a spreadsheet application such as *Microsoft Excel®.*

Instructions:

1. Students will launch a spreadsheet. Explain the meaning of a cell on a spreadsheet and how to name each cell, such as A1 or C8.
2. Students will be creating a formula on the computer that will calculate multiplication facts.
3. Students will begin in cell A2 and enter the numbers 1–12 going down.
4. Students will then enter the number 1 in cell B1.
5. Have students click on B2 and explain to students that you want the computer to multiply Cell A2 with cell B1. Discuss with students how a spreadsheet formula always starts with the equal sign. So in cell B2, the formula should be = B1 * A2
6. Students will then click on B3 and enter their formula (= B1 * A3). Notice when a student presses enter, the answer of the multiplication facts goes into the cell. Students will continue this process of entering formulas until they are finished.
7. Once they have entered the formulas, students will click on cell B1 and change the number to 7 or 9. Once the students press enter, they can watch all of the other numbers compute. Change the number in B1 again to 57 or 83. Watch the computer calculate.

Extension Ideas:

Students enjoy watching the computer do math problems instantaneously. Students may want to make a class budget or calculate ticket sales for a musical on a spreadsheet. Students could then make graphs based on this information.

Using Formulas on a Spreadsheet *(cont.)*

Calculating Multiplication Tables

Step 1
Enter numbers

	A	B	C
1		1	
2	1		
3	2		
4	3		
5	4		
6	5		
7	6		
8	7		
9	8		
10	9		
11	10		
12	11		
13	12		
14			
15			

Step 2
Enter formulas

	A	B	C
1		1	
2	1	=B1*A2	
3	2	=B1*A3	
4	3	=B1*A4	
5	4	=B1*A5	
6	5	=B1*A6	
7	6	=B1*A7	
8	7	=B1*A8	
9	8	=B1*A9	
10	9	=B1*A10	
11	10	=B1*A11	
12	11	=B1*A12	
13	12	=B1*A13	
14			
15			

After the formula is entered, press return. Then the formula will change to the answer of the multiplication problem. Once all formulas are entered, change the number in B1 to a higher number and watch all the answers change.

Pictures on a Bar Graph

Objectives:

- Understanding basic spreadsheet skills
- Entering data into spreadsheet cells
- Making a bar graph with labels
- Copying and pasting appropriate pictures

Application Needed:

Students will need a spreadsheet application such as *Microsoft Excel*®. In addition, students will need clip art available.

Instructions:

1. Students should research the speeds of animals to see how fast they can run and add that data to a chart.
2. Students will open a blank spreadsheet.
3. Students will enter data.
4. Students will highlight data and make a bar graph.
5. Students should add an appropriate title and labels. Explain to students about the X-axis and Y-axis. Have them label the correct axis with "miles per hour" depending on if the bars are horizontal or vertical.
6. Students should change the color of the bars.
7. Students will then find pictures that correspond to each animal and copy and paste them to the graph.
8. Graphs should be proofed and then printed.

Extension Ideas:

Ask students to research speed of cars. Information can be found at this website: **http://www.teachercreated.com/url-updates/2448-2**. **Click on page 46, site 1**. Students may want to make a double bar graph comparing car speeds with animal speeds. You could broaden the topic to have students research the speeds of other forms of transportation. For example, airplanes, trains, or space shuttles. If students finish early, have them make math problems with the information. For example, "If an airplane and a train both traveled 100 miles at their top speed, approximately how much earlier would the airplane arrive than the train?"

Pictures on a Bar Graph *(cont.)*

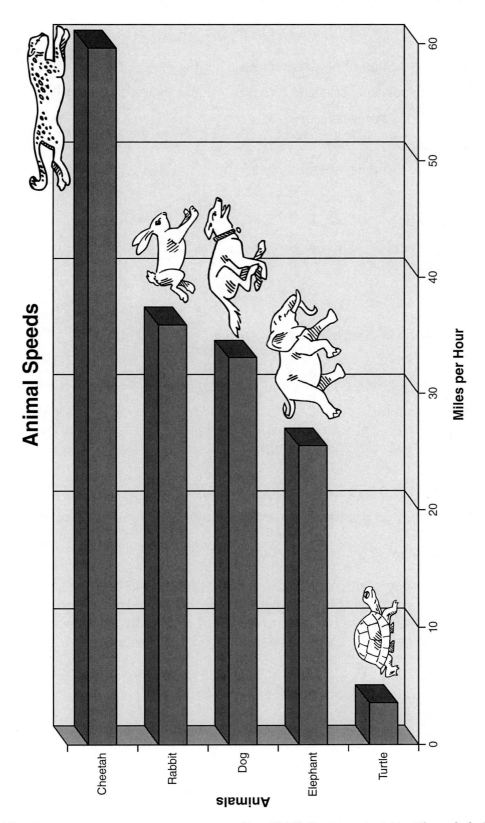

More Pie (Charts), Please

Objectives:

- Understanding the basics of a spreadsheet
- Becoming familiar with spreadsheet terms
- Highlighting cells in a spreadsheet
- Making a pie chart
- Changing colors of the different sections

strawberry	11
orange	13
lemon	7
grape	11
lime	12

Application Needed:

A spreadsheet application will be necessary for this project, such as *Microsoft Excel*®. Clip art should also be available.

Instructions:

1. Distribute a package of Skittles® to each student or pair of students.
2. Have students count how many of each flavor of Skittles® that they have.
3. Students will open the spreadsheet and enter data similar to that in the chart shown above.
4. Once the data is entered, students should highlight the 10 cells with information in them and make a pie chart. The chart should include the name of each flavor and the percent represented. Discuss with students how the computer changed their numbers into percents.
5. Students can change the color of each piece of pie.
6. Students should add an appropriate title and clip art and print their work.

Extension Ideas:

This idea will work with any candy which is easily countable. Halloween is a good time to do this project because you can buy large bags of candy that have multiple miniature bags in them. This way each student can have his or her own bag of candy. You may want to encourage students to research the national color distribution of Skittles® or another candy and make two pie graphs for comparative purposes.

More Pie (Charts), Please (cont.)

Flavor Distribution in My Pack of Skittles®

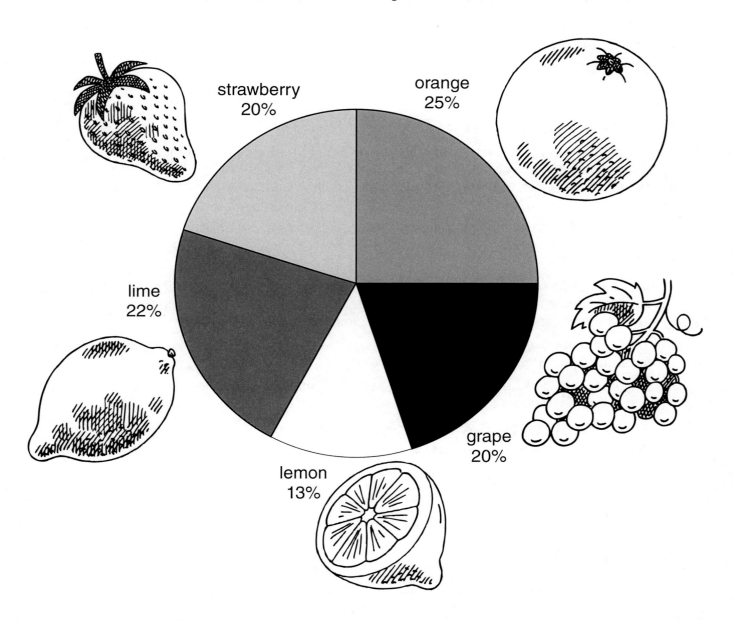

Input Internet Information

Objectives:

- Using and understanding the basic functions of the Internet
- Understanding a basic spreadsheet
- Knowing terms such as cell, *X-axis*, and *Y-axis*
- Entering data into a spreadsheet

Application Needed:

Students will need access to the Internet.

You will need Internet access because you will be finding pen pals on the Internet. There are always schools eager to become partners on the Internet. Websites like *The Teachers Corner* offer free pen pal services that will connect you with other classes similar to yours across the world.

To make this graph, use an application that has a spreadsheet capability.

Instructions:

1. You will need to set up pen pals for your students ahead of time. Launch the Internet and go to **http://www.teachercreated.com/url-updates/2448-2. Click on page 50, site 1**. Follow the instructions for finding available classrooms.
2. Discuss this weather project with your Internet pen pals. This particular graph compares temperatures in three US cities for one week.
3. Have each school collect their temperature data—the high temperature for their particular city in a designated week.
4. In column A, enter the names of the cities. See the example below.
5. In row 1, enter the days of the week.
6. Enter the temperature data in cells B2 through F4.
7. Use the data to create a graph. A bar or line graph works the best.
8. Add a chart title, X-axis title, and Y-axis title.

	A	B	C	D	E	F
1		Monday	Tuesday	Wednesday	Thursday	Friday
2	Norfolk, VA	20	18	17	21	23
3	Orlando, FL	29	31	33	35	38
4	Chicago, IL	5	5	7	6	4

Extension Ideas:

You could graph any type of data related to weather, such as cloud formations, barometric pressure, or average precipitation.

Input Internet Information *(cont.)*

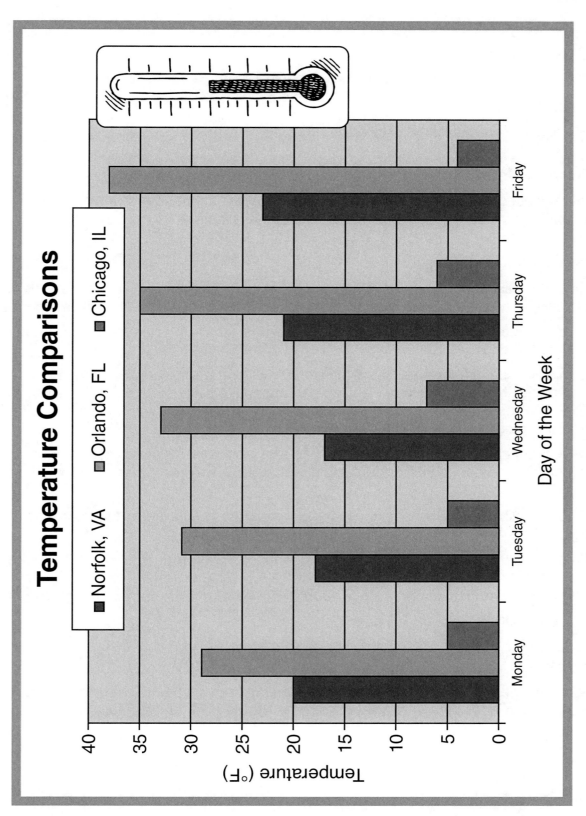

Research Report

Objectives:

- Using two programs at the same time
- Reading material and typing it in their own words
- Using a template
- Becoming more familiar with Internet addresses

Application Needed:

Students will need access to the Internet and an application that allows you to draw boxes and type inside the boxes. Clip art should also be made available.

Instructions:

1. Students will need to open a web browser and the program in which you have designed the template. Upper-level students can make the template themselves if time permits.

2. Students will go to **http://www.teachercreated.com/url-updates/2448-2 and click on page 52, site 1.**

3. In this website, students will research wolves, looking particularly for information about wolf packs, hierarchy, communication, and pups. Help students gather facts while reading about wolves, then go back to the open template and type the information in the first box. (Remind students to write it in their own words.)

4. Have students go back to the wolf website and read about communication. Students will remember one or two interesting facts about wolf communication and type them on the template.

5. Students will continue this process until all boxes are full, including the Interesting Facts box.

6. Students will add a title and pictures. Students can add pictures from a CD-ROM or from the Internet. The following are good websites for wolf pictures. **http://www.teachercreated.com/url-updates/2448-2. Click on page 52, sites 2, 3, and 4.**

7. Students will spell-check and print.

Extension Ideas:

Teachers can follow up their wolf research by reading a novel about a wolf, such as *Julie of the Wolves* or *White Fang*. Students could also make drawings of the wolf-pack hierarchy.

Research Report *(cont.)*

WOLVES

The Pack Hierarchy

Wolves are very intelligent and sociable. They live in organized packs of 5–10 similar type animals. In most wolf packs there is a leading pair called the alpha male and female. The alpha pair leads the pack during the hunt and makes necessary decisions.

Communication

Wolves howl for many different reasons. Howls can be used to locate a lost member of the group or help encourage pack unity.

Their Pups

A female wolf usually has a litter of 3–10 pups in the spring. These pups are small, weighing about one pound. The mother tends to her pups while the wolves in the pack care for the mother.

Interesting Facts

1. Wolves can smell their prey over a mile away.

2. Wolves can run 5 mph for long periods of time but have been known to sprint as fast as 35 mph.

3. Often times it takes the strength of the pack to kill large prey such as a deer or caribou.

Search Engines

Objectives:

- Understanding search engines
- Becoming familiar with website addresses
- Learning how to find valuable facts from the Internet
- Improving general Internet browsing skills

Application Needed:

Students will need access to the Internet.

Instructions:

1. Students will launch the Internet browser and go to a search engine. One can type in a subject and find Internet sites about that topic. There are several search engines, such as Google (**http://www.teachercreated.com/url-updates/2448-2. Click on page 55, site 1**) or Yahoo! (**http://www.teachercreated.com/url-updates/2448-2. Click on page 55, site 2.**)

2. Once the students have launched their search engines, have them type their subject matter in the search box.

3. They will then see how many sites met the search (often times the number will be well over 1,000). Usually the best sites are in the first 25 or 30.

4. Have students find information on a city or country in Europe. To find flight prices, your students may want to go directly to an airline website: (**http://www.teachercreated.com/url-updates/2448-2. Click on page 55, site 3.**)

5. Students will continue to find information about their city or country, such as popular foods, currency, weather, and fun facts and record it on pages 55–56. Students may want to go to the *Weather Channel* (**http://www.teachercreated.com/url-updates/2448-2. Click on page 55, site 4**) to find the weather for their European countries.

6. Students should write the web address of the site next to the fact. Explain how important it is to cite where they found their information.

Extension Ideas:

European Internet research is great to do in conjunction with the travel brochure (see pages 105–107). One can also research any city or country around the world. If students are doing state or country reports, require them to use at least two Internet sites as sources.

Search Engines *(cont.)*

http://www.teachercreated.com/url-updates/2448-2
Click on page 55, site 1, 2, 3, or 4.

Date: _____ Name: _____

Name of City or Country: _____

Hotels: _____

_____

Flight Prices: _____

_____

Attractions: _____

_____

_____

_____

Popular Foods: _____

_____

Currency & Exchange Rate: _____

_____

Search Engines *(cont.)*

Weather: _____

_____

Shopping: _____

_____

Fun Facts

1. _____

_____

2. _____

_____

3. _____

_____

4. _____

_____

5. _____

_____

Virtual Tour

Objectives:

- Locating a specific website on the Internet
- Scrolling up and down in a website
- Clicking forward and backward in a website
- Scanning through information on the Internet to find specific facts
- Drawing meaningful conclusions from Internet articles

Application Needed:

Students will need access to the Internet.

Instructions:

1. Students will launch a web browser and go to *The Virtual Body* website at **http://www.teachercreated.com/url-updates/2448-2. Click on page 58, site 1.**

2. Students will see the four sections of the body (heart, digestive tract, brain, and skeleton). Students will be navigating through these four sections to find the answers to the questions on the following pages.

3. Show students how to scroll up and down in a website. Demonstrate to students how to move forward and backward in the website.

4. Students will then scan through the *Virtual Body* website to find the answers to the questions on pages 58–59.

5. Once everyone is finished, discuss the answers as a class.

6. If time permits, show the students other human body websites. Look at the website addresses listed below.

Extension Ideas:

The human body is a fascinating subject. There are many other wonderful websites to explore such as the following two:

http://www.teachercreated.com/url-updates/2448-2. Click on page 57, site 1, 2.

Teachers may want to combine graphing with the lesson. Have students measure their resting heart rates and record them. Then have students run in place for one minute before taking their heart rates again. Have students record the data and graph the differences.

Virtual Tour *(cont.)*

The Virtual Tour of the Body

http://www.teachercreated.com/url-updates/2448-2
Click on page 58, site 1

Date: _____   Name: _____

Use this website to answer the following questions.

1. Click on **The Human Brain**. Scan through the articles to find an interesting fact about each of the following:

   A. Headaches: _____

   _____

   B. Goosebumps: _____

   _____

2. Go back to the main page. Click on **Digestive Tract**. Take the guided tour. Find two facts on how the digestive system works.

   A. _____

   B. _____

3. Go back to the main page. Click on the **Human Heart**. Scan through the list of articles. Name two parts of the heart and describe what they do.

   A. _____

   _____

   _____

   B. _____

   _____

   _____

Virtual Tour (cont.)

4. What causes the "dub-dub" sounds that the heart makes?

_____

_____

_____

5. Go back to the main page. Click on **Skeleton**. Click on the **Zoom-in**. Roll your mouse cursor over the skeleton to see close-up views of the bones. Write the location of the following bones:

mandible: _____

tibia: _____

occipital bone: _____

femur: _____

metacarpal bones: _____

humerus: _____

ulna: _____

6. Return to **http://www.teachercreated.com/url-updates/2448-2 and click on page 59**, **site 1**. Read this article to find two interesting facts about sports injuries.

A. _____

_____

B. _____

_____

Determining Distance

Objectives:

- Typing a specific website address and finding the site
- Reinforcing basic map skills
- Building a world-wide awareness of cities

Application Needed:

Students will need access to the Internet.

Instructions:

1. Students will launch the Internet.
2. Have students go to the *Geodistance* website at
   http://www.teachercreated.com/url-updates/2448-2 and click on page 61, site 1.
3. Students will then be able to click on two cities and find the distance between them. This will work not only nationally but internationally, too.
4. Have students click on the city or state where they live.
5. Next have students click on Seattle, Washington.
6. Have students look at the top left-hand corner of their screen; the distance is listed in miles. Have them record the distance and then click on yards, feet, km, and meters. Record the distances.
7. Have students click on another city. This will create a new leg from Seattle, Washington. Record the distance.
8. Students can clear the entire route to complete the activity. They can also undo the last leg of their route to go back a step. Students may need to refresh the page to change the scale of the map.

Extension Ideas:

This website is one to bookmark for a point of reference because of its usefulness. A teacher could base a whole math lesson around this website. For instance, students could be asked to find five pairs of United States cities, all of which are about the same distance apart (give or take 20 miles).

While reading a class novel, it may be interesting to note exactly how far the main character traveled from point A to point B. Science students could investigate exactly how many miles Monarch butterflies migrated last fall from their point of origin to Mexico.

Determining Distance (cont.)

http://www.teachercreated.com/url-updates/2448-2
Click on page 61, site 1

Launch an Internet browser and type the above address for *Geodistance*. Use the plus and minus symbols in the top left-hand corner of the map to change the scale of the map. You may also use the arrows to move the map in any direction.

1. Click on the city where you live. Now click on Seattle, Washington. Look for the distance at the top left-hand corner of the page.

   Record the distance in miles (mi): _____

   yards (yd): _____

   feet (ft): _____

   kilometers (km): _____

   meters (m): _____

2. Click on **Clear Entire Route** on the right-hand side, and then click on Los Angeles, California. Next click on District of Columbia (Washington, DC).

   Record the distance in miles: _____

3. Click on the map to show a route that starts in Chicago, Illinois with a leg to Denver, Colorado, and another leg from Denver to Dallas, Texas.

   Record the total distance: _____

4. Imagine you live in Lincoln, Nebraska and you are going to visit your grandmother in Orlando, Florida, but first you have to visit your uncle in Jackson, Mississippi.

   How many miles do you travel in total? _____

   How many less miles would you travel if you went straight to Orlando from home?

   _____

5. How many miles is it from your home state to Morocco? _____

6. Two friends from Russia are traveling to the United States, one to the West Coast and one to the East Coast. Map their routes. Do they take the same route? _____

7. Click on **Find A Route**. Find the Golden Gate Bridge and click on it.

   How long is the bridge? _____

8. Click on **Find a Route**, click on **Next** until you find Broadway tip to tip, New York.

   How long is Broadway? _____

9. Map a route from your city to Ensenada, Mexico, with one stop in between. List the city in which you stop before you go to Ensenada. _____

   What is the distance between your city and the first stop on your route? _____

   What is the total distance of your route? _____

Determining Distance *(cont.)*

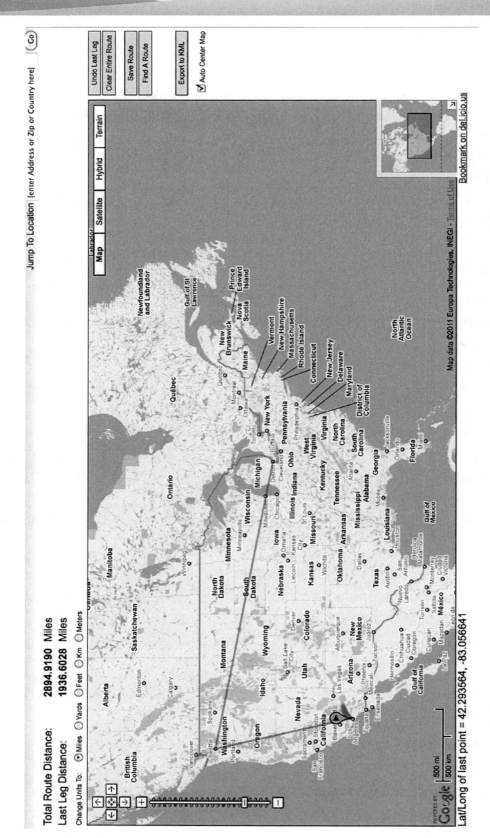

Map It!

Objectives:

- Typing a specific website address and finding the site
- Understanding basic Internet terms such as World Wide Web
- Reinforcing basic map skills

Application Needed:

Students will need access to the Internet.

Instructions:

1. Students will need to know the street addresses of their school, home, and a friend or relative who lives out of town.

2. Students will launch an Internet browser.

3. Have students go to the *Google Maps* site at **http://www/teachercreated.com/url-updates/2448-2 and click on page 63, site 1.**

4. Students will get a map of their school and its surrounding areas. To do this, have students type the address of their school in the space provided, and then click on **Search Maps**.

6. Once students see this map, then they can zoom in and out to get different views. Allow students to experiment. Talk to them about roads or highways that are north or south of the school. Have them decide which direction it is to each of their homes.

7. Click on **Get Directions**.

8. Now have students type their personal addresses as the origin address (A) and the school's address as the destination (B). Then click on Get Directions.

9. This will show a possible route to school for each student. Next have them go back and keep the origin address of their house but change the destination address to that of an out-of-town friend or relative, or a specific destination.

Extension Ideas:

Google Maps is a valuable resource for many curriculum subject areas. Teachers could have large maps in which students could highlight routes from one point to another. In addition, students can discover how many miles it is from one city to another or from school to home.

Math teachers could have students find how many MORE miles it is from Chicago to Dallas than Chicago to St. Louis. This also can be a useful website in Driver's Education Class.

Map It! *(cont.)*

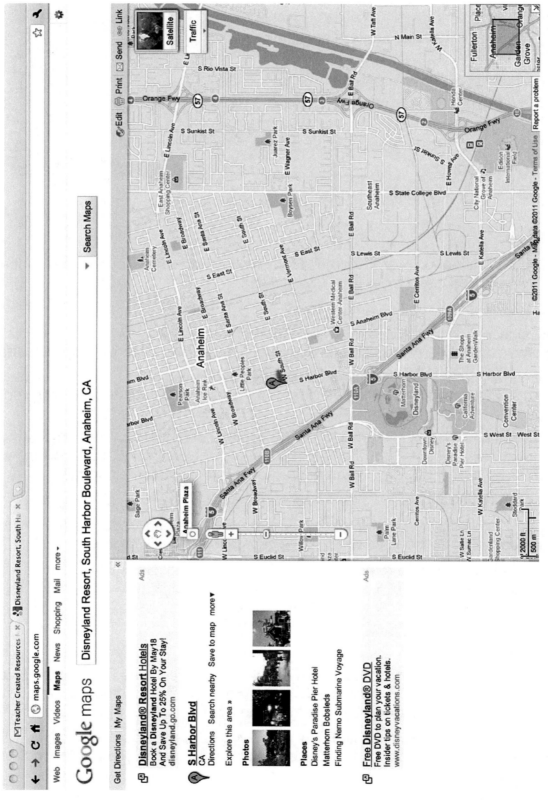

Map It! *(cont.)*

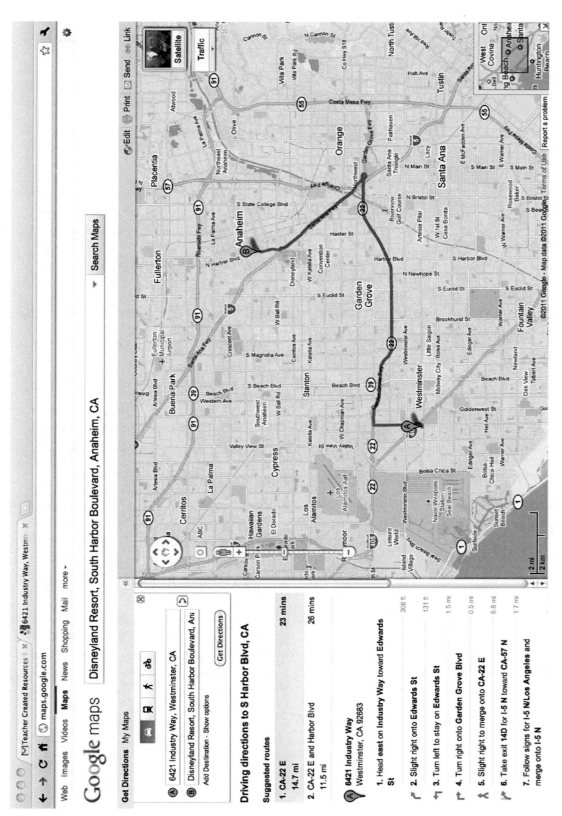

Worldwide Weather

Objectives:

- Learning the meaning of website addresses
- Becoming successful with finding specific information on the Internet
- Using up, down, back, and forward arrows
- Learning Internet terms such as website, home page, Internet browser, etc.

Application Needed:

Students will need access to the Internet.

Instructions:

1. Students will launch the Internet.
2. Students will go to *The Weather Channel* site:
   (**http://www.teachercreated.com/url-updates/2448-2. Click on page 67, site 1.**)
3. Students will type the name of their city or of a large city near their house, and then click on FIND WEATHER.
4. Students will browse through the website to find the answers to the questions on pages 67–68 using the up, down, back, and forward, arrows.
5. Students will find the current temperature and present humidity in their city.
6. Students will check to see when is the best day for a barbecue in the next week.
7. Students will look at the Doppler radar to find any precipitation in their city.
8. Students will look at the travel conditions in their city and check on flight delays across America.
9. Students will visit international cities and compare temperatures.

Extension Ideas:

This lesson is a great one to use when studying weather and making weather maps and charts. See pages 50–51 to get ideas about weather graphs. The Internet is full of wonderful websites. Go to a search engine and type your subject matter. You will probably find many sites related to your subject and then you could make up a worksheet similar to the one on pages 67–68.

Worldwide Weather *(cont.)*

Date: _____   Name: _____

http://www.teachercreated.com/url-updates/2448-2
Click on page 67, site 1

Launch the Internet and type the above address for *The Weather Channel*. Browse through this website to answer the following questions.

Type the name of your city and click **FIND WEATHER**.

1. What is the current temperature in your city? _____

2. What is the present humidity in your city? _____

   Do you consider this high or low? _____

3. How many minutes ago was the information updated? _____

4. If you were planning an outdoor BBQ in the next five days, which day or days would be best according to the weather? _____ or

   _____

   Click on the **Maps** tab and then click on **Doppler Radar**.

5. Is there any rain in the entire beige area? _____

6. Do you think your city has a chance of getting rain in the next 24 hours according to the Doppler radar? _____

   Click on the **BACK ARROW**. Find the current temperature for Honolulu.

7. Is Honolulu warmer or cooler than your city right now? _____

   By how many degrees? _____

Complete this table.

	Your City	Chicago	Phoenix	Boston
Tomorrow's High Temp.				
Tomorrow's Low Temp.				

Worldwide Weather (cont.)

Click on the **Forecasts** tab and then click on **Pollen Forecast**. Type in your city or zip code.

8. Is your city experiencing a high level of pollen? _____

9. Why do you think this may be? _____

   _____

Click on the **Travel** tab and then click on **Flight Tracker**. Select your state from the pull-down menu and select an airport.

10. What is the weather and temperature at the airport? _____

    _____

11. How many minutes delay are they currently experiencing at

    the airport? _____

Click on the **Weather Apps** tab. Type Paris, France and type in Phoenix, Arizona.

12. According to **Weather At-a-Glance**, how many degrees cooler is Paris than Phoenix on average?

    _____

13. List the records shown in the **Weather At-a-Glance** box.

    _____

Complete this table with the forecasted high temperatures in these cities.

	Paris, France	Kiev, Ukraine	Calcutta, India	Your Choice _____
Tomorrow's High				

Finding and Using Clip Art

Objectives:

- Finding clip art on the Internet
- Copying and pasting pictures from the Internet
- Typing extemporaneously
- Using more than one program simultaneously (multitasking)

Application Needed:

You will need access to the Internet in addition to an application that will allow you to paste pictures, type extemporaneously, and move items around on the page.

Instructions:

1. Launch the Internet. Go to **http://www.teachercreated.com/url-updates/2448-2. Click on page 69, site 1.**

2. Have students pick a snowman on the page.

3. To copy an image from the Internet, right-click on it and then click "Copy Image." The image may also be dragged to the desktop.

5. Open the computer software application you're using for the project (do not close the Internet), and click on Edit, then Paste. That section of the snowman should appear and students can move it where they want it.

6. Now students are finished working on the Internet and can close it.

7. Students will then create a math word problem related to their snowman. Students should end their statements with a question mark, add a blank line for the answer.

8. Work should be spell-checked and proofed. Allow students to print their pages when they can give the correct answers to their problems.

Extension Ideas:

In addition to writing a math word problem, students could each write a short story about their snowman. Another cute idea would be for each student to write a poem entitled "Ingredients for a Snowman."

Finding and Using Clip Art *(cont.)*

Billy the snowman was sitting in his front yard watching cars pass. In one hour he saw 8 cars pass by his house. If this pace continues, how many total cars will Billy see in 9 hours?

Finding Information on the Net

Objectives:

- Understanding search engines
- Becoming familiar with website addresses
- Understanding when websites are updated
- Understanding the size of websites
- Understanding the meaning of the World Wide Web
- Learning how to gain valuable facts from the Internet

Application Needed:

Students will need access to the Internet.

Instructions:

1. Students will launch a search engine and go to **http://www.teachercreated.com/url-updates/2448-2 and click on page 72, site 1 or site 2.**

2. Once the students have launched their search engines, have them type their subject matter in the search box.

3. You will then see how many sites meet the search. Often the number will be well over 1,000. (Usually the best sites are in the first 25 or 30.)

4. Read the site summaries. Notice when it was last updated. (If a student is doing something on a current crisis, you don't want to choose a site that was updated a year ago.)

5. Also have the students look at the size of any documents they want to launch or download. The larger the file, the longer the download time. If time is of importance, limit the size of the document that can be launched or downloaded.

6. Once students find a site that they like, they can begin researching. The following page is a format that students can use. Be sure to have the students include their Internet website addresses and explain the importance of citing sources.

Extension Ideas:

Students can research just about any topic on the Internet. This lesson would be a good time to explain to students the difference between fact and opinion.

Finding Information on the Net *(cont.)*

Internet Research

Date: _____   Name: _____

http://www.teachercreated.com/url-updates/2448-2
Click on page 72, site 1 or 2.

Topic: _____

Website Address: _____

_____

Facts From the Internet:

1. _____

_____

_____

2. _____

_____

_____

3. _____

_____

_____

Insects on the Internet

Objectives:

- Locating Internet addresses on the computer
- Scanning through information to find facts
- Typing facts in boxes and adjusting box size
- Copying and pasting appropriate clip art

Application Needed:

Students will not only need access to the Internet but also an application in which they can paste clip art and draw boxes and lines. *Microsoft PowerPoint®* presentation software will work well for this project.

Instructions:

1. Students will go to **http://www.teachercreated.com/url-updates/2448-2 and click on page 73, site 1.**

2. Students will choose insects to research. Students will navigate through the insect website and take notes on four insects. Discuss with students the importance of not copying straight from the Internet but putting their findings in their own words.

3. Once students have enough notes on each insect, have them begin their projects on the computer by creating four large text boxes on their pages.

4. Students will type their facts in each box. Facts should be in full sentences and form a paragraph. Font size should probably be 14–16 point.

5. Once students have typed all of their information, they may need to enlarge or shrink the box to fit all of their information comfortably. Students may also need to shrink the font if information still does not fit.

6. Students should find appropriate pictures of their four insects either from a CD-ROM or the Internet.

7. Work should be proofed, spell-checked, and then printed.

Extension Ideas:

As a follow-up to this lesson, students may want to find one or two more websites about their four insects. Students could also make a matching game with their facts and pictures. Students could cut out their pictures and fact boxes, and have friends match them together.

Insects on the Internet *(cont.)*

Monarch butterflies are insects. They are poisonous to birds that eat them. They get their poison from the milkweed they eat. Monarchs travel south to migrate in the fall. The male monarch has dots on both wings.

Dragonflies can fly at incredible speeds and then stop almost instantaneously. Their special eyes help them to do this. Instead of having one lens, their eyes have thousands of lenses which allow them to view wide areas, hunt for prey, and fly more accurately.

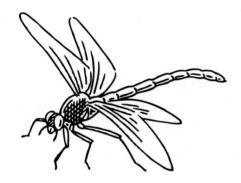

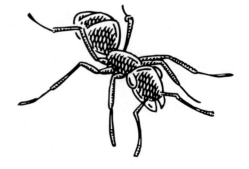

Ants are very social animals and live in groups called colonies. Colonies may have fifty or so members. Super colonies have been reported to have thousands of workers in nests connected to each other.

Bees are very important to our environment. They carry pollen from plant to plant on their wings. This process is called cross pollination. The bees' biggest defense mechanism is their stinger. Bee stings can be quite painful and swell up in size.

Animals on the Internet

Objectives:

- Locating a specific website on the Internet
- Scrolling up and down on a web page
- Scanning through information on the Internet to find interesting facts
- Writing Internet facts in your own words

Application Needed:

Students will need access to the Internet.

Instructions:

1. Students will launch the Internet and go to **http://www.teachercreated.com/url-updates/2448-2 and click on page 76, site 1** to visit SeaWorld/Busch Gardens ANIMALS.

2. Once SeaWorld is launched, students will click on Animal Info on the left-hand side.

3. Next, students will click on ANIMAL BYTES and a long list of animals will appear.

4. Students will scroll through the list and choose five different animals. Once students have clicked on an animal, they should scroll down to FUN FACTS. Students should read through these FUN FACTS and rewrite one in their own words. Stress how important it is to not copy directly from any source but to put facts into their own words.

5. When students finish, they can draw their five animals on the back of the fact sheet. Or, another part of this website can be explored.

Extension Ideas:

Teachers may ask students to look over their fact sheets and choose one of their five animals on which to write an extensive animal report. Students could then be asked to use a search engine on the Internet (Google or Yahoo!) and find two more websites that have information on their animals.

Animals on the Internet *(cont.)*

Date: _____   Name: _____

http://www.teachercreated.com/url-updates/2448-2
Click on page 76, site 1.

Then click on Animal Info on the left side. Next, click on **ANIMAL BYTES**.

Find 5 animals on the list. Scroll down to the **FUN FACTS** and write an interesting fact about each animal.

Animal #1: _____

    Fact: _____

_____

Animal #2: _____

    Fact: _____

_____

Animal #3: _____

    Fact: _____

_____

Animal #4: _____

    Fact: _____

_____

Animal #5: _____

    Fact: _____

_____

Computing Cost

Objectives:

- Finding websites on the Internet
- Successfully navigating through a website
- Reinforcing math skills
- Discovering the vast resources on the Internet

Application Needed:

Students will need access to the Internet.

Instructions:

1. Students will go to **http://www.teachercreated.com/url-updates/2448-2 and click on page 77, site 1.**
2. Next, have students click on BROADWAY on the left-hand side under Listings/Tickets.
3. Then have students click on a show they would like to see.
4. Have students read about the show and click on the button where it says BUY TICKETS.
5. Students can compute how much it would cost for a family of four to see a certain show on a particular day. Students can compare show prices and plan an entire trip to Broadway for a family.
6. Students can also close the purchasing window and go back to the main page to find national touring shows or a list of shows in a specific city.
7. Students can print and use information.

Extension Ideas:

Playbill.com is a useful website to bookmark. When students are doing city or state reports, it would be nice to include entertainment available in the city.

Math teachers can make entire lessons based on this website, such as, "How much more would it cost a family of four to see *Sound of Music* in the lower level compared to balcony seats?"

Computing Cost *(cont.)*

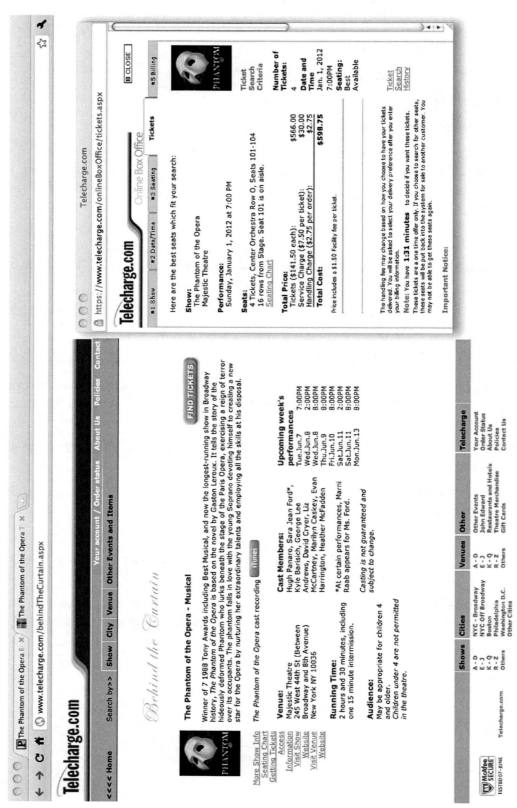

Researching History 1

Objectives:

- Typing a specific website address and finding the site
- Copying and pasting Internet pictures into another application
- Understanding basic Internet terms such as World Wide Web

Application Needed:

You will need access to the Internet and any word processing application, such as *Microsoft Word*®.

Instructions:

1. Have students launch the Internet. Explain the meaning of a web address. If time permits, show students other Internet addresses, such as **http://www.usatoday.com** or **http://www.nfl.com.**

2. Students will go to **http://www.teachercreated.com/url-updates/2448-2 and click on page 79, site 1.**

3. Students will scroll down and read about hieroglyphs and their meaning.

4. Students will open a blank word-processing page and type a paragraph about the meaning of hieroglyphs in their own words.

5. Have students go to **http://www.teachercreated.com/url-updates/2448-2 and click on page 79, site 2**. Type in their name using the keyboard at the bottom of the screen.

6. Have students copy each of their hieroglyph letters onto their word processing document. To copy and paste an Internet picture, simply right click on the picture. A pull down menu will appear; click on COPY IMAGE. Then launch *Microsoft Word*® and click on Edit, Paste. The image may also be dragged to the desktop.

7. Print the word processing page that includes the hieroglyphs.

Extension Ideas:

Students can write entire messages in hieroglyphs and e-mail them to pen pals or friends.

You could also consult with an art teacher and have your students draw their names in hieroglyphs or create their own set of hieroglyphs.

Researching History 1 *(cont.)*

The Meaning of Hieroglyphs by Megan

Hieroglyphs were an ancient way of writing begun by the Egyptians. In this language, symbols equaled letters or objects. They did not have any punctuation or spaces in between words. The Egyptians had several hundred different symbols. Egyptians did not normally write with vowels, thus only the consonants remained in a word.

Egyptians were interested in their appearance and enjoyed the decorative style of their language. Often, the hieroglyphs were artistically carved and painted on an Egyptian temple or tomb.

The Rosetta Stone, discovered in 1799, was a piece of granite with a message written in three different languages including hieroglyphs.

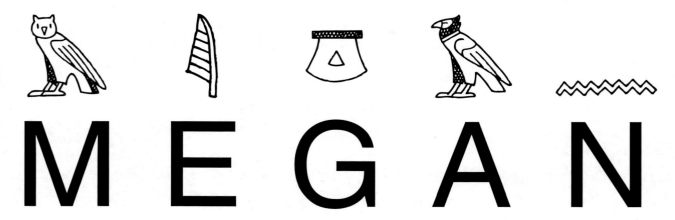

M E G A N

Researching History 2

Objectives:

- Typing a specific website address and finding the site
- Copying and pasting Internet pictures into another application
- Working with more than one program at the same time

Application Needed:

Students will need access to the Internet and an application in which they can draw boxes and type in the boxes such as *Microsoft Word®*.

Instructions:

1. Students will launch the Internet. If time permits, show students other Internet addresses such as **http://www.disney.go.com/index** or **http://www.weather.com**.

2. Go to **http://www.teachercreated.com/url-updates/2448-2 and click on page 81, site 1** to visit National Geographic's travel website.

3. The students will open a blank Word document.

4. Students will draw boxes, label the boxes in a way that is similar to those on the next page (pyramids, hieroglyphs, mummies, etc.).

5. Students will go back into the Internet and find facts about pyramids.

6. Students will open their pages with the boxes and rewrite their facts about pyramids in their own words. Students will continue going back and forth between programs until all boxes are completed.

7. Have students copy and paste pictures from the Internet page to fill in blank areas. To copy and paste an Internet picture, simply right click on the picture. A pull-down menu will appear; click on COPY IMAGE. Then launch *Microsoft Word®* and click on Edit, Paste. The image may also be dragged to the desktop. Have students notice on the Student Sample page that the website from which the photos were found is credited.

8. Spell-check and print the completed page with the boxes on it.

Extension Ideas:

Students can make fact sheets like this Egypt one with any subject matter. This is also a great way for students to share how they celebrate the holidays.

Researching History 2 *(cont.)*

Egypt Facts by Taylor

Pyramids

Pyramids were graves for the Egyptian kings. The Egyptians thought the pyramids honored the king and protected him from any harm.

Mummies

A mummy is a dead body that is preserved in a special way so the body doesn't rot. The tradition of mummification was overseen by the priests in Egypt.

Hieroglyphs

An important breakthrough for the understanding of hieroglyphs was the discovery of the Rosetta stone in 1799. The stone is a piece of black granite with the same writing written in three different scripts, one script being hieroglyphs.

Other Facts

1. The stem of the papyrus plants was used to make Egyptian paper.

2. The Egyptians primarily ate bread and drank beer. Skeletons show their teeth were worn down by the bread they ate. Their beer was thicker and more nutritious than beer today.

3. Egyptians were quite concerned about their appearance. They wore makeup, perfume, and fine garments.

Visiting National Parks

Objectives:

- Becoming more confident on the Internet
- Scanning through information to find facts
- Drawing boxes and lines
- Typing facts in boxes and adjusting box size

Application Needed:

Students will not only need access to the Internet but also an application in which they can paste clip art and draw boxes and lines. *Microsoft PowerPoint*® will work well for this project.

Instructions:

1. Find a blank map of the United States on a CD-ROM or another clip art application. Have the students copy and paste this map on the *PowerPoint*® page.

2. Students will go to **http://www.teachercreated.com/url-updates/2448-2 and click on page 83, site 1**.

3. Students should scan through this website and find facts on 4–7 national parks.

4. Students will also need to identify the exact location of each national park they have chosen. Students will attach a box to the line. In each box students will identify the park and write a fact about it.

5. Students will spell check their work and print.

Extension Ideas:

The study of national parks is great for a social studies unit. In addition to doing the map, students could find the distance between each park. Students can go to the *Geodistance* website (**http://www.teachercreated.com/url-updates/2448-2. Click on page 83, site 2**) to find the distance between national parks. Teachers may want to expand this project and have students organize a trip including transportation, lodging, and attractions. It would be wise to assign a maximum number of miles traveled and a limit on budget. Students could then make a poster showing their travel route and include details about transportation, lodging, and attractions.

Visiting National Parks *(cont.)*

Visiting National Parks *(cont.)*

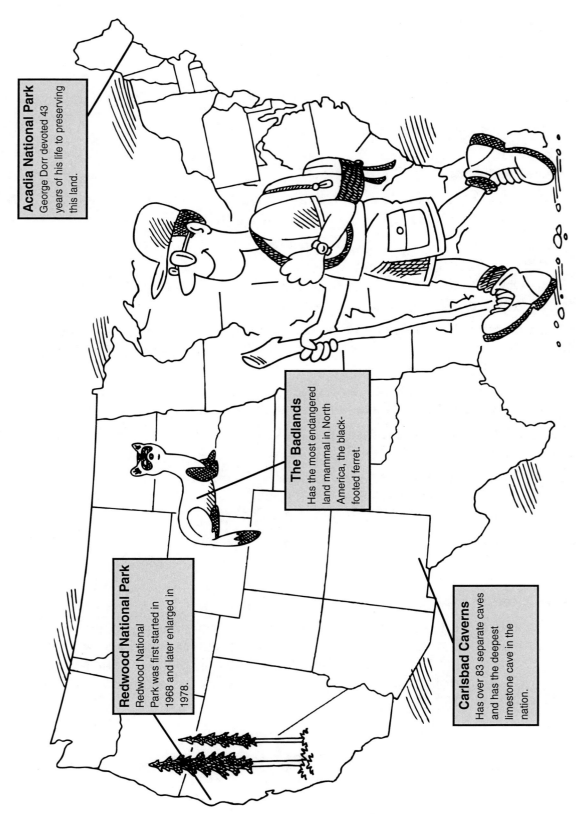

Acadia National Park
George Dorr devoted 43 years of his life to preserving this land.

The Badlands
Has the most endangered land mammal in North America, the black-footed ferret.

Redwood National Park
Redwood National Park was first started in 1968 and later enlarged in 1978.

Carlsbad Caverns
Has over 83 separate caves and has the deepest limestone cave in the nation.

Finding Pictures

Objectives:

- Using search engines such as Google and Yahoo!
- Finding specific pictures on the Internet
- Copying pictures from the Internet
- Pasting pictures into a different application

Application Needed:

Students will need access to the Internet and an application in which they can paste their pictures such as *Microsoft Word*® or *Microsoft PowerPoint*®.

Instructions:

1. Students will go to **http://www.teachercreated.com/url-updates/2448-2 and click on page 87, site 1 or site 2** to launch a search engine.

2. Once the students have launched their search engines, have them type what sort of picture they want, such as a human heart or a panda bear. Use the following page to guide their search.

3. They will then see how many sites met their search (often times the number will be well over 1,000). Usually the best sites are in the first 25 or 30.

4. Students will then click on a website that looks good and find one of the pictures from the list.

5. To copy and paste a picture from the Internet, right click on the picture. A menu box will appear and click on COPY IMAGE. Open another application and paste picture on a blank page. The image may also be dragged to the desktop.

6. Students will continue this process until they have all of the pictures on the list or until time expires.

Extension Ideas:

Students often like to use Internet pictures for projects. Understanding how to find appropriate pictures on the Internet is a valuable skill. If students are studying a particular unit such as Washington, DC, a teacher may want the students to find only pictures pertaining to Washington, DC. Another extension idea would be for students to find pictures of American-made products on the Internet.

Finding Pictures *(cont.)*

Date: _____   Name: _____

Can You Find These Pictures?

Use a search engine to find the pictures in the list below.

http://www.teachercreated.com/url-updates/2448-2
Click on page 87, site 1 or site 2

Check off the pictures you find. Copy and paste the pictures into another program.

_____ panda bear

_____ human heart

_____ Mickey Mouse

_____ a computer

_____ a dinosaur

_____ Native American

_____ USA flag

_____ McDonald's trademark arches

_____ whale

_____ famous actor/actress

_____ any US president

_____ tornado

_____ camera

_____ the Golden Gate Bridge

_____ clouds

_____ butterfly

_____ golfer

Top News Stories

Objectives:

- Locating a specific website on the Internet
- Successfully navigating through a web page
- Scanning through information on the Internet to find specific facts
- Drawing meaningful conclusions from charts and graphs

Application Needed:

Students will need access to the Internet.

Instructions:

1. Go to **http://www.teachercreated.com/url-updates/2448-2 and click on page 89, site 1.**

2. Using a hard copy of today's *USA TODAY* paper, show students the similarities between the hard copy and the Internet. Discuss the different sections of the newspaper at the top of the website (i.e. Sports, Money, Life, Weather). Show students how these are the same as the hard copy. (Other newspapers may be used, too, as long as they have websites as well.)

3. Demonstrate to students how to navigate through a website to find valuable information. Students will then begin to answer the questions on the following pages.

4. Have students complete the Top News Stories student page and discuss the answers as a class.

Extension Ideas:

Students may want to work in small groups and create a mini newspaper of their own. Discuss the making of a newspaper, not only the articles, but headlines, pictures, etc. In addition to *USA Today*, there are many other newspapers and magazines online. Have students locate *Time* magazine (**http://www.teachercreated.com/url-updates/2448-2. Click on page 88, site 1**) and read the cover story of the most recent issue.

Top News Stories *(cont.)*

Date: _____   Name: _____

http://www.teachercreated.com/url-updates/2448-2
Click on page 89, site 1

Answer the following questions by navigating through this website.

1. Date of Newspaper: _____

2. Top news headline of today: _____

   _____

3. Read the lead article in the **Life** section and create a new headline for it:

   _____

   _____

4. Did the stock market go up or down? _____

5. What is the major sports headline for today?

   _____

   _____

Top News Stories *(cont.)*

6. Click on the **Weather** tab. Click on the **Maps** scroll-down menu and select **Temperatures**. Name two cities or states experiencing 60-degree temperatures today.

_____   _____

7. Which U.S. regions are expecting precipitation today?

_____

8. Browse the different sections and find an article that contains an opinion.

What is the headline? _____

What is the opinion? _____

9. On the front page of the USA TODAY paper, scroll down to the USA Snapshot. Explain this picture graph in your own words. (If you are not using USA TODAY, describe another picture on the page.)

_____

_____

White House Scavenger Hunt

Objectives:

- Working with the Internet
- Understanding Internet terminology
- Understanding website addresses
- Learning navigation skills for the Internet

Application Needed:

You will need access to the internet.

Instructions:

1. Give students a general overview of the Internet and demonstrate its vast capabilities.

2. Share with students basic Internet terminology, such as "World Wide Web," "URL," "home page," and navigation terms specific to your choice of Internet software.

3. Write the White House's website address on the board (**http://www.whitehouse.gov**) and explain to students what each portion of the address refers to. Explain how this website address is different than the White House's street address, 1600 Pennsylvania Avenue.

4. Students should type in the White House website address and begin a scavenger hunt. Assist students with the first few questions to get them going. (There are two versions: Beginner and Intermediate.)

5. Once students are finished with the scavenger hunt, they may e-mail the president or another member of the White House staff. In the event that your students do not have personal e-mail accounts you may choose to e-mail the president as a class using the teacher's e-mail address.

Extension Ideas:

Scavenger hunts are wonderful ways to perfect students' Internet skills while they learn pertinent facts about a particular subject. There are many great websites on which you could base a scavenger hunt. By the completion of this scavenger hunt, students should possess the basic skills needed to use the Internet as a powerful research tool.

White House Scavenger Hunt *(cont.)*

Date: _____   Name: _____

http://www.whitehouse.gov

or

http://www.teachercreated.com/url-updates/2448-2
Click on page 92, site 1

Click on the **ADMINISTRATION** tab.

1. What is the name of the current president? _____

2. What is the name of the first lady? _____

3. The name of the vice president is _____.

Click on the President's name.

4. The President was born in the state of _____.

5. The President is the _____ President of the United States.

White House Scavenger Hunt *(cont.)*

6. Does the President have any children? _____

7. When was the President born? _____

Go to **http://www.teachercreated.com/url-udpates/2448-2 and click on page 93, site 1.**

Click on **FIRST PETS**. Answer the following questions.

8. Does the President have any pets? If so, what are they?

   _____

9. What type of animal is Socks? _____

10. President Johnson had two beagles named _____

    and _____.

11. Old Whiskers was a _____.

12. Fala, the best loved and most famous of all First Pets, belonged

    to _____.

Click on **Contact Us** in the upper right-hand corner. You may e-mail someone in the White House.

White House Scavenger Hunt *(cont.)*

Date: _____   Name: _____

Internet Scavenger Hunt of the White House

http://www.whitehouse.gov/about/history

or

http://www.teachercreated.com/url-updates/2448-2
Click on page 94, site 1

Answer the following questions.

1. _____ chose the site to be the capitol which is called Washington, DC today.

2. When did the construction of the White House begin? _____

3. Who was the architect? _____

4. Did George Washington ever live in the White House? _____

5. _____ was the first President to live in the White House.

6. Was the White House ever on fire? _____ When? _____

7. There are _____ rooms in the White House.

8. The White House has _____ floors.

9. At various times in history, the White House has been known as

   _____.

10. _____ officially gave the White House its current name in 1901.

White House Scavenger Hunt (cont.)

http://www.teachercreated.com/url-updates/2448-2
Click on page 95, site 1

Take an interactive tour of all the rooms and answer the questions below.

1. What objects are in the Vermeil Room? _____

2. Were any of the books on display in the Library written by foreign authors?

    _____

3. Who was the original First Lady to begin using the China Room to display the
    pieces of china and glass used by past presidents? _____

4. Which room is the largest in the White House? _____

5. Which president used the Green Room as a dining room?

    _____

6. How was ice cream introduced into the White House?

    _____

7. What shape is the Blue Room? _____

8. How many guests can the State Dining Room sit for dinner or lunch?

    _____

How do you think a first pet spends its day? Write down three or four things you
think that a first pet does that regular pets might not do during the day. Use the
back of this sheet to write your answer.

Fact or Fiction?

Objectives:
- Using the Internet as a research tool
- Typing a specific website address and finding the site
- Successfully navigating a website
- Gaining knowledge about sharks

Application Needed:
Students will need access to the Internet.

Instructions:
1. Students will go to **http://www.teachercreated.com/url-updates/2448-2 and click on page 97, site 1.**

2. Have students read through this website and discover facts and myths about sharks.

3. If time permits, have students find one other address of a shark website. To do this, students would need to go to a search engine and type "sharks." Have students write down the address of this website and write two or more interesting facts about sharks. To explore a variety of shark behaviors, anatomy, and realities, go to **http://www.teachercreated.com/url-updates/2448-2 and click on page 97, site 2.**

Extension Ideas:
Ocean life is a popular subject matter for many grade levels. There are wonderful sites on whales, dolphins, and other marine life. The following websites will be useful to you for further research on marine life.

http://www.teachercreated.com/url-updates/2448-2. Click on page 96, sites 1, 2, and 3.

Fact or Fiction? *(cont.)*

Date: _____   Name: _____

Go to http://www/teachercreated.com/url-updates/2448-2 and click on page 97, site 1.

Fact or Fiction?

Circle the statements that are **facts** in the list below.

1. Sharks are mammals that have been around long before the dinosaurs existed.

2. Sharks have no bones. Their skeleton is made of cartilage.

3. Half of the 369 shark species are over 39 inches (1m) long.

4. No surfer has ever been attacked by a shark.

5. Scientist have demonstrated that sharks are able to learn at a rate similar to that of white rats and pigeons.

6. Whale sharks are harmless whales.

7. Tiger sharks will eat anything — fish, mammals, birds, and even other sharks.

Great White Shark Facts:

Write two interesting facts about great white sharks that you found while researching on the Internet.

1. _____

2. _____

Tiger Shark Facts:

Write two interesting facts about tiger sharks that you found while researching on the Internet.

1. _____

2. _____

On the back of this sheet, draw a picture of a shark similar to the one pictured on this website.

The Planets

Objectives:

- Locating Internet addresses on the computer
- Scanning through information to find facts
- Typing facts in boxes
- Copying and pasting appropriate clip art

Application Needed:

Students will need access to the Internet and an application in which they can paste clip art and draw boxes and lines. *Microsoft PowerPoint®* will work well for this project.

Instructions:

1. Go to **http://www.teachercreated.com/url-updates/2448-2 and click on page 98, site 1.**

2. Give each student one planet to study. Students will be navigating through this website to find particular facts on their planets, such as distance from the sun, length of day, composition of the atmosphere, temperature, and diameter.

3. Depending on the skill level and the time allotted, the teacher or students will make a template with seven text boxes similar to the one on the next page.

4. Students will title these boxes "Average Distance From the Sun," "Temperature," etc. The last box should be fairly large and be entitled "Fun Facts."

5. Students will type their information. Once students have typed all of their information in a box, they may need to enlarge or shrink the box to fit all of their information comfortably. Students may also need to shrink the font if information still does not fit.

6. Students will then find appropriate pictures either from a CD-ROM or the Internet.

7. Student's work should be proofed, spell-checked, and then printed.

Extension Ideas:

As a follow-up to this lesson, students may want to find one or two more websites about their planet. Students may want to expand the Fun Facts box onto another page to fit 6–10 other facts. Students could print two copies of the fact page. With the extra copy, students can cut each of their fun facts into strips. Students can place these facts into a bin. The teacher could pull out one fact, read it, and have students guess which planet it is.

The Planets *(cont.)*

FACTS ABOUT: MERCURY

**Average Distance
From the Sun:**
36,000,000 miles

Length of Day: 59 Earth Days

Temperature: -300°–870° F

**Composition of the
Atmosphere:**

Oxygen
and
Helium

Diameter at the Equator:

3,032 miles

Fun Facts

1. Mercury has the shortest year of all the eight planets.

2. Earth's year is 4 times longer than Mercury's year.

3. Mercury is so hot that it could melt lead.

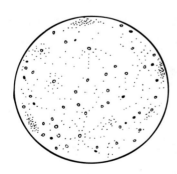

All About Me

Objectives:

- Using presentation software
- Making attractive slides
- Working with bulleted text
- Building text
- Making transitions between slides
- Adding clip art
- Viewing slide shows and rehearsing the timing

Application Needed:

Use a presentation application that has all of the capabilities listed in the objective list above. *Microsoft PowerPoint*® is an excellent application to use for this project. For younger elementary children, *KidPix*® will get them familiar with the concepts but will not be as professional in appearance as *Microsoft PowerPoint*®.

Instructions:

1. Open the presentation application. Consult the manual or help menu for specific questions related to the application you have chosen.
2. Choose a background that will be used for all of the slides. Students can change the color of each slide, but the background should be uniform.
3. Make a title slide entitled "The Life of . . ."
4. The title of slide #2 should be "Three Interesting Facts About Me."
5. The title of slide #3 should be "Three Future Goals of Mine."
6. Under Format, change the color of each slide.
7. Change the font style, font color, and font size on each slide.
8. Add suitable clip art from the application or copy and paste clip art from another application.
9. Build the bulleted points. (This means that each point will appear one at a time when you are making the presentation.)
10. Using the Format menu, make transitions between slides.
11. View the slide show and rehearse the timing.

Extension Ideas:

Students could add more slides to their slide shows using ideas such as hobbies or sports. With some presentation software, animation can also be added.

This lesson was designed to teach students the basic skills needed to successfully use presentation software. The possibilities are endless for presentation ideas. This is a great way to present any information, especially book reports or science projects.

All About Me *(cont.)*

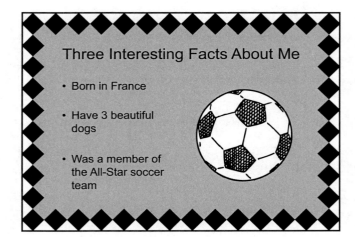

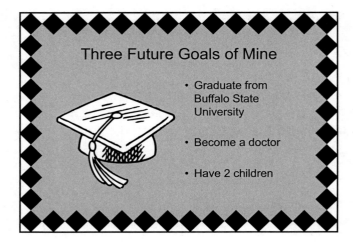

MY POWERPOINT PRESENTATION

PowerPoint® Projects

Objectives:

- Learning the basics of presentation applications such as *Microsoft PowerPoint*®
- Making bulleted text
- Resizing clip art objects
- Learning techniques for attractive layout design

Application Needed:

Use an application that is geared toward presentation. *Microsoft PowerPoint*®, which is one component of the *Microsoft Office Suite*®, is an excellent source. Many educators do not realize how easy *PowerPoint*® is to use because it is primarily popular in the business world. Another set of applications that will work are in *Adobe Creative Suite*®.

Instructions:

1. Students will research a topic and find several interesting facts about the subject.
2. Students will then open *Microsoft PowerPoint*®. Choose Format if you want to have a color design or just leave as is if you want to make a project more like the panda bear project shown on the next page.
3. Next, have students choose the layout that has a title, three points, and a clip art picture.
4. Have the students type their title in the title bar. One may change font size, style, or color by highlighting the title and using the tool bar at the top.
5. Next, have your students click on the first bullet and type their first fact (do not press return until you are finished with the first fact).
6. After the first fact, press return to get another bullet. Have the students type the rest of their facts. Highlight facts and adjust their size as needed.
7. Add clip art from *Microsoft PowerPoint*®, a CD-ROM, or the Internet. Print.

Extension Ideas:

Beginning and intermediate computer students enjoy making *PowerPoint*® projects because of the professional results. Projects can relate to the curriculum and/or holidays. Parents and grandparents love to hear why they are appreciated, and this is a nice way to display it.

PowerPoint® Projects *(cont.)*

Panda Bear Facts

- Panda bears usually weigh between 165–350 pounds.

- Their teeth are made to chew bamboo, their favorite food.

- A panda bear has poor vision.

- A panda bear's sense of smell is very good.

- Male pandas are slightly larger than the females.

- Brown and white pandas exist but are extremely rare.

Happy Mother's Day

- I love it when we bake my birthday cake together and decide new ways to frost it.

- Thank you for taking me to all of my tennis practices and matches.

- I appreciate all of the times you take care of me when I am sick.

Designing Travel Brochures

Objectives:

- Learning basic desktop publishing skills
- Inserting borders
- Formatting text in different fonts
- Inserting pictures from a CD-ROM or the Internet

Application Needed:

Use a desktop publishing application such as *Microsoft Publisher*® or *Adobe PageMaker*®. This lesson will take more than one class period and will require students to possess intermediate computer skills.

Instructions:

1. Students should choose a particular country or city to make a travel brochure. Students need to gather facts about this city from the Internet or other sources. See pages 71–72 for Internet research help.

2. Students will create a two-sided travel brochure with three columns on each side. (You may want students to draw a quick sketch of their travel brochure with pencil and paper. Have students practice folding their rough drafts to make sure information is in the desired location.)

3. Students will then make text boxes and type information in them adhering to the three-column format.

4. Students will also add pictures from a CD-ROM or from the Internet in appropriate boxes.

5. Tell students that changing fonts, sizes, and colors will enhance a travel brochure tremendously. Also, putting borders around text will give it more of a professional appearance.

6. Spell-check and proof the brochure and then print.

Extension Ideas:

Travel brochures are great to teach during a foreign language class or as a culminating project for a social studies unit. In addition, students could create a brochure advertising a project, company, or invention. If your school hosts an invention fair, a three-panel informative brochure would be a nice addition to a regular invention project.

Sara's Travel Brochure on Paris

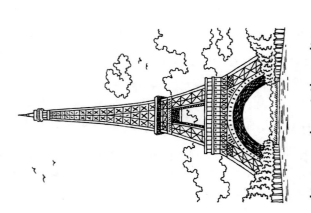

Learn about the city everyone wants to visit.

Paris, France

The City of Lights

Paris, the "City of Lights," has a legendary atmosphere of romance that is found on busy streets, at cozy sidewalk cafes, and in quiet public gardens, offering your group the kind of ambiance that is indispensable to the success of your meeting.

Importantly, you will also find thousands of hotels and world-class meeting facilities. With over 950 conventions a year, Paris has been the world's convention capital for the past 12 years.

As for dining, there is almost complete unanimity of opinion that French cuisine is the best in the Western World, and you will find it available in 5-Star restaurants as well as in many of the smaller bistros.

Designing Travel Brochures *(cont.)*

Shopping and Dining in Paris

Fashion is a huge French industry and shoppers will enjoy browsing through designer shops carrying the latest Paris trends. Shop windows are beautifully arranged making window shopping a national pastime. Some of the best shopping areas are along the Left Bank, Place de la Madeleine, and the Louvre's Palais Royal. The exchange rate is 0.6926 Euros to one U.S. dollar. Using credit cards is advisable since many credit card companies can offer you a better exchange rate.

The main passion is French food and wine. The country's culinary techniques are respected internationally. Favorites are mushrooms, cheeses, breads, seafood, lamb, and pâté de foie gras.

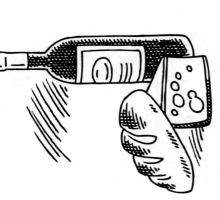

The Friendly Skyline℠
UNITED AIRLINES

Nonstop flights from Chicago to Paris daily!

Low rates!

1-800-555-4321

Les Halles

Rent your own apartment while in Paris! Enough room for the whole family! Includes kitchen.

Call: 1-800-555-1234

Paris' Most Popular Attractions

Thousands visit Paris each year to see its famous museums, monuments, and theme parks. Le Louvre could be the most world-renowned art gallery. Its enormous collection includes the *Mona Lisa* and the *Venus de Milo*.

The internationally recognized symbol of France is the 1,063 ft. Eiffel Tower, built during 1887–1889. Visitors should check out the Musee de l'Homme, the Musee de Monuments, the National Popular Theater and the National Film Library, all located at the Tower's base.

Disneyland Paris happens to be France's most popular tourist attraction, with twice as many visitors as the Eiffel Tower or Le Louvre.

Flow Charts

Objectives:

- Learning the basics of an organizational chart
- Inserting boxes into an organizational chart
- Formatting text in different fonts
- Putting borders around boxes

Application Needed:

There are several applications one can use to make a family tree. *Microsoft PowerPoint*® has an organizational chart feature that can be used to make family trees or flow charts. However, there are programs specifically designed to make family trees that can be purchased as well.

Instructions:

1. Students need to research their family genealogy at least 2–3 generations back.
2. Students will open *Microsoft PowerPoint*® and choose a blank presentation document.
3. Students will go to **Format** and click on **Slide Layout**. Choose the organizational chart layout.
4. Students will click on the top box and type their name in it.
5. Students will click on the boxes going down and type their parents' names. To delete boxes, click on a box one time and press delete on the keyboard.
6. Students can add more boxes going across or down by clicking on the co-worker (box will go across) or subordinate (box will go down).
7. Students should continue adding their family tree information until all necessary boxes are filled.
8. To change font, font color, and box color, have the students select all of the boxes (Edit, Select All). Then go to the Menu bars and make changes.
9. Once the family tree is completely finished, have the students click on File, then Save. After saving, students may then close the file.
10. The family tree will automatically be put in on the *Microsoft PowerPoint*® page. Students can resize it by clicking on the blank handles and pulling out.
11. Add pictures and title.
12. Print.

Extension Ideas:

Family trees make nice gifts to parents or grandparents. Making flow charts is also a great way to perfect these skills. If improving skills is the goal, choose a subject that the students already know the steps involved, such as "The Steps to Make a Peanut Butter and Jelly Sandwich."

Flow Charts *(cont.)*

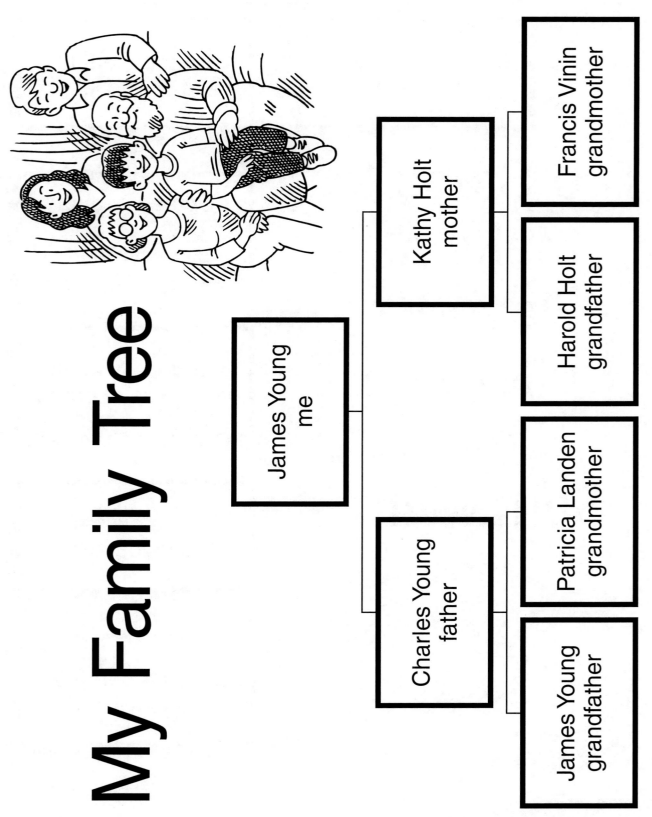

My Family Tree

James Young
me

Kathy Holt
mother

Charles Young
father

Francis Vinin
grandmother

Harold Holt
grandfather

Patricia Landen
grandmother

James Young
grandfather

Flow Charts (cont.)

Get out two slices of bread.

Get out peanut butter and jelly.

The Steps to Make a Peanut Butter and Jelly Sandwich

Spread peanut butter on one slice of bread.

Spread jelly on the other slice of bread.

Put the pieces of bread together.

Eat your delicious sandwich.

Creating Bookmarks

Objectives:

- Understanding the rulers and margins on a document
- Enlarging font size
- Changing font style and color
- Accessing pictures from a CD-ROM
- Understanding correct proportions for a document

Application Needed:

Use a drawing application that is flexible but can also make professional looking documents. *Microsoft Publisher*® or applications in *Adobe Creative Suite*® will work well.

Instructions:

1. Students will be creating bookmarks as a culminating project for a book report. Prior to making the bookmarks, students will need to be well acquainted with their books and the themes represented.

2. Give students the dimensions of the bookmarks, such as 6" x 3" (15 cm x 8 cm) and show them how to use the rulers provided for them on the computer.

3. Students should include the title of their book and the author.

4. Students should also include freehand artwork and/or clip art to represent themes in the book.

5. Proof the final product and then print. (Consider printing on card stock if your printer will handle the stiffness of the paper.)

6. Laminate the bookmarks. Have students share them with the class and tell them about the significance of the artwork, colors, etc.

Extension Ideas:

A teacher could run a contest for the best bookmark, which could be voted on by students or faculty members. If the whole class is reading the same novel, consider having each student or pair of students choose a scene to depict from the novel. These could be displayed on a bulletin board in chronological order.

In addition to making bookmarks related to book reports, students could make bookmarks related to subject matter, such as writing their names in hieroglyphs.

NUMBER THE STARS

BY
LOIS LOWRY

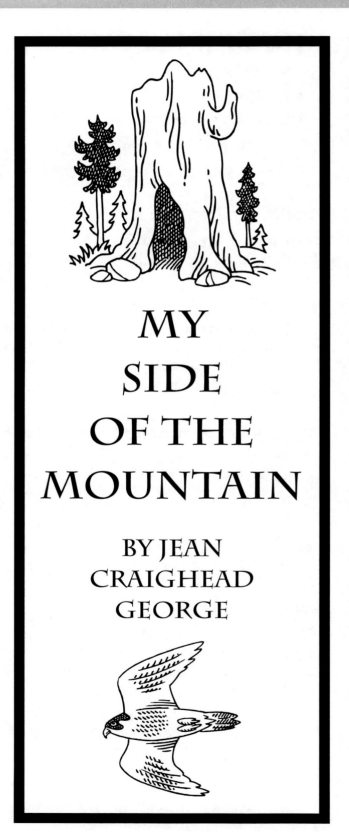

MY SIDE OF THE MOUNTAIN

BY JEAN CRAIGHEAD GEORGE

Creating Bookmarks *(cont.)*

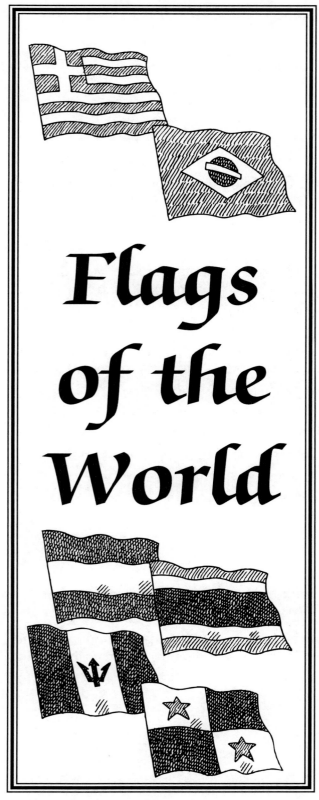

Scientific Illustration

Objectives:

- Drawing objects freehand on the computer
- Drawing lines with arrows on the ends
- Typing sentences in particular locations
- Spell-checking information

Application Needed:

Use a good drawing application that allows students to type. Suggestions include *HyperStudio*®
or *Microsoft Publisher*®.

Instructions:

1. Students will be studying fish and possibly other sea life. Students should have a good understanding of the basic parts of a fish. If they do not, explain the parts of a fish to them. (Encyclopedias have good information on the basic parts of a fish and details about each part.)

2. Have students draw a large fish with the basic features (eye, mouth, gills, top fin, back fin, scales, and pectoral fin) filling most of their pages. Upper-level students may want to draw a fish showing more parts.

3. Draw a line pointing out each basic part. It would be preferable for students to put an arrow at the end of each line, either by freehand or with the application being used.

4. Students will then write 2–4 sentences about each part. They may have learned this information in class or found it on the Internet or in a book.

5. Students should then spell-check and proofread their work.

6. Finally, have students print their work.

Extension Ideas:

For a follow-up to this lesson, students may want to color their fish with markers or colored pencils.

Drawing diagrams is a great way for students to organize information they have learned. There are many other items that could be diagrammed, such as parts of the heart, layers of the skin, features of a volcano, or parts of a leaf. If pictures are really difficult to draw, a teacher may want to consider allowing students to use pictures from a CD-ROM.

Scientific Illustration *(cont.)*

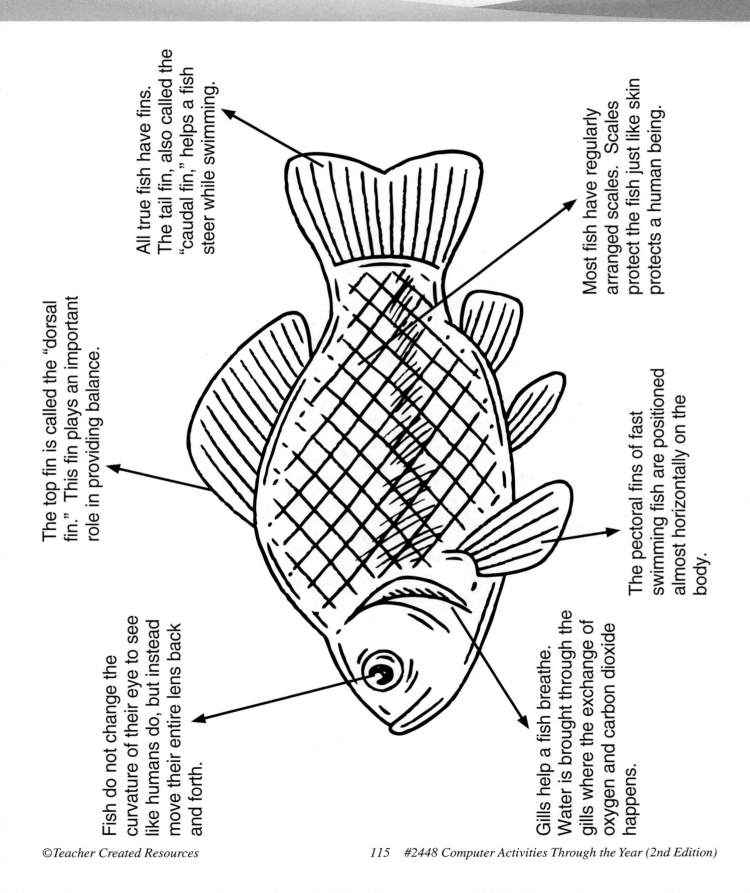

All true fish have fins. The tail fin, also called the "caudal fin," helps a fish steer while swimming.

Most fish have regularly arranged scales. Scales protect the fish just like skin protects a human being.

The top fin is called the "dorsal fin." This fin plays an important role in providing balance.

The pectoral fins of fast swimming fish are positioned almost horizontally on the body.

Fish do not change the curvature of their eye to see like humans do, but instead move their entire lens back and forth.

Gills help a fish breathe. Water is brought through the gills where the exchange of oxygen and carbon dioxide happens.

Creating Cards

Objectives:

- Perfecting clip-art skills
- Learning the basic double-fold card
- Adding a border
- Grouping text and pictures together
- Rotating or flipping grouped objects

Application Needed:

Use an application that has the capability to make a border, group objects together, and flip objects. *Microsoft Word*® and *Microsoft Publisher*® work well for this exercise.

Instructions:

1. Make a copy of the example card on the next page.

2. Fold it twice so it makes a card.

3. Show students how the folded card looks, compared to the full sheet. Point out the four quadrants on the full page, like the example on the right.

4. On the computer, have students make a page with four quadrants. (If you already have an application that has a card format, use that.)

5. Students will then fill in the quadrants with text and pictures. (Adding a border to the front of the card makes it look more professional.)

6. Remember that anything put in the "Inside Right" or the "Inside Left" quadrants must be flipped upside down. See the example on the next page.

7. Finally, have students remove any quadrant guidelines before printing.

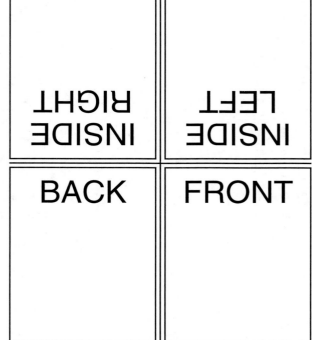

Extension Ideas:

These are basic instructions for any card. Students could make birthday cards for nursing home residents as an act of community service. This is also a nice way to say thank you to a room mother or a field-trip speaker. Sending Internet pen pals a card is always fun for children. One could also use card making as an incentive. Once a student is finished with his or her work, he or she could use the classroom computer to make a card for a friend or relative.

Creating Cards *(cont.)*

*You are very
special to me.
Thanks for all the
fun things you do
with me.*

Handcrafted
by Heather

Grandma
&
Grandpa

Making Flags

Objectives:

- Adding lines, circles, and other designs on the computer
- Filling areas with color
- Understanding symmetry

Application Needed:

Use an application such as *Microsoft Word*® that allows the students to add circles, squares, lines, and other shapes. In addition, students should be able to add color.

Instructions:

1. Discuss with students different types of flags. Give them examples of flags that have stripes, circles, pictures, patterns, etc. Students may want to make an existing flag for a country report, or the teacher may have the students design a flag on their own.

2. Have students add the basic rectangle shape on the computer.

3. Students will then decide on a basic design for their flags. They can create circles, stripes, stars, etc. Students will then design their flags.

4. Students should add color to various parts of the flag.

5. You may want to have students write paragraphs about their flags. Students should include the reasons why they chose a particular design, the meaning of the color scheme, or the name of their country.

6. Students' work should be proofed and then printed.

Extension Ideas:

Students may want to research nautical flags, create nautical flags, and write about the usage of each nautical flag. If the school is near a body of water, you may want to organize a field trip to the harbor and talk to sailors or the Coast Guard about nautical flags. In addition, students may want to research famous flags, such as the United Nations flag, and discuss their origination and symbolism.

Making Flags *(cont.)*

Barbados

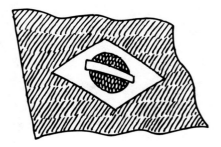

Brazil

Egypt

Greece

Malaysia

Norway

Panama

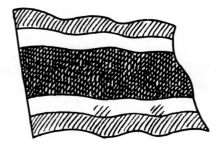

Thailand

Uganda

Coupon Gifts

Objectives:

- Adding text
- Resizing clip art
- Rotating text
- Orienting the page to landscape
- Adding borders
- Duplicating items on the computer

Application Needed:

Use an application that has an extensive clip art gallery and a variety of borders available. The application should also have the capability of adding text, changing fonts and color, and rotating text.

Instructions:

1. Show students how to set up the page and printer to landscape.
2. Choose a border from this application or a CD-ROM and add it on, sizing it so that it fills a quarter of the page.
3. Copy and paste it three times. Change the color of the other borders if desired.
4. Add text and clip art to create four coupons. (If your students are beginners, have them write their four ideas for coupons on scrap paper first. Then edit these ideas before the students type them on the computer.)
5. Demonstrate how to rotate text to make coupons look more attractive.
6. Change colors of text.
7. Add appropriate clip art from a CD-ROM or another application.
8. Finally, proofread, spell-check, and print.

Extension Ideas:

Parents always enjoy homemade gifts from their children. These coupons make a lovely present for any holiday. For an added touch, students could send these coupons in the mail to their parents. Also, instead of coupons, students could use this same idea to make tickets for a class play or carnival.

Coupon Gifts *(cont.)*

This coupon is good for serving you breakfast in bed.

This coupon is good for cleaning up my room! (one time)

This coupon is good for washing your car.

This coupon is good for watching Judy for 2 hours.

Word Art

Objectives:

- Learning other applications within a word-processing application
- Setting margins and paper size
- Perfecting toolbar skills
- Choosing style and direction of text
- Changing fonts and resizing text
- Adding borders

Application Needed:

Use a word-processing application in which you are able to make word art. There are many applications that have this capability, such as *Microsoft Word*® or *Microsoft Works*®. Try to choose an application in which you can add a border to your word art, too.

Instructions:

1. Students should open the word-processing application.
2. Set up the page to be landscape or portrait, depending on the word art idea.
3. Maximize paper size by making all margins smaller.
4. Locate the word art function within the program. All the programs will probably have it in a different place. Consult the Help Menu to find the location.
5. Type in the text for the word art.
6. Using the toolbar, change the style and direction of your text.
7. Using the toolbar change the font and size.
8. Finally, add a border and print.

Extension Ideas:

This is a great lesson to use at the beginning of the school year as an ice breaker. Often times a student's word art reflects his or her personal interests. Word art could also be pasted on a notebook cover or book report. Students will also enjoy making word art for their cubby, locker, or bedroom door.

Word art makes a nice Teacher Appreciation Day gift, like the example on the next page.

Teachers can make quick and attractive signs for their bulletin boards, too.

Kelsey's Room

Mr. Smith's Classroom

Harrison College
Harrison College
Harrison College

Barstow's Sluggers

Door Hangers

Objectives:

- Adding text
- Resizing clip art
- Changing the outline of the text to a different color than the inside fill color.
- Setting up the page to portrait
- Perfecting overall computer skills

Application Needed:

Use an application that has an extensive clip-art gallery and allows you to change fonts and color. Try to find an application that already has the outline of a door hanger available. If you are unable to find an application that has this, you could scan in a picture of the door hanger. Or, students could draw it freehand on the computer screen using the application's drawing tools.

Instructions:

1. Find an outline of a door hanger.
2. Show students a variety of finished door hangers to give them an idea of your expectations. See the examples on the next page. Emphasize to students that the pictures should relate to the message.
3. Add pictures and text.
4. Change the outline of the text to a different color so the text is two-color.
5. Before printing, make sure your page is set to portrait. You can do this by going into the Printer Setup or Page Setup, depending on the program. Setting it up for portrait means that your page will print up and down instead of width-wise. (You want your door hanger to be long and thin, not short and wide.)

Extension Ideas:

This would be a great way to get to know your students at the beginning of the year. Students could also make door hangers for their bedroom doors that describe themselves.

Door Hangers *(cont.)*

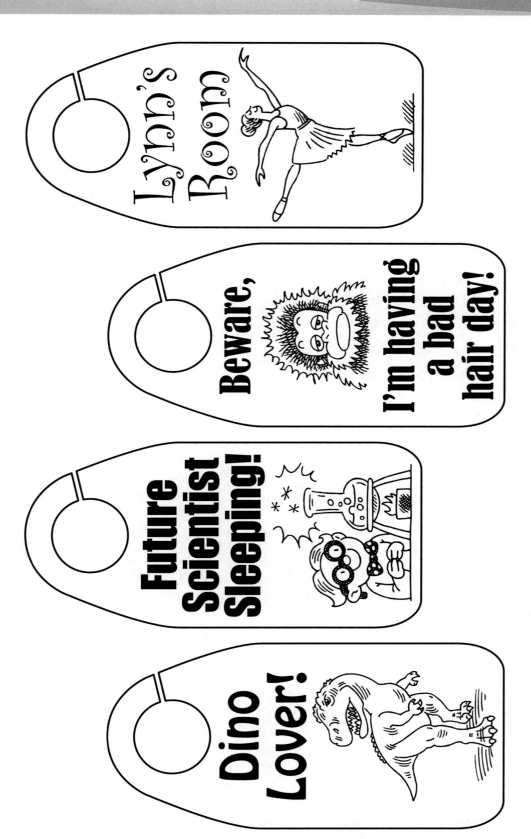

Illustrating Quotes

Objectives:

- Changing fonts and colors
- Resizing pictures
- Perfecting typing skills

Application Needed:

Use an application that has an extensive clip-art gallery and allows you to change fonts and color. *Microsoft Word*® works for this exercise.

Instructions:

1. Students should pick a quote or an interesting fact that has to do with the space industry. (Try to make it so everyone in the class has a different quote or fact.)
2. Type the quote, reviewing basic typing skills.
3. Change the font, font size, and color.
4. Add pictures that relate to the quote or fact. Resize the pictures to fit on the page nicely.
5. Students should site their reference for the quote or fact on the page.
6. Print the students' work. (This page would look great pasted on a class report or project.)

Extension Ideas:

Quotes from famous artists, musicians, or athletes would work nicely, too. The main goal for this lesson is to teach students how to enhance reports and projects. Students could make a fact sheet on a particular subject area, such as dinosaurs or butterflies. This would also be a good time to stress that students need to document their sources.

Another way to use this idea is for morning exercises. Each day a different student could share a thought-provoking quote of the day. The student would be required to do it on the computer. You could make an attractive bulletin board with all of these quotes.

Illustrating Quotes (cont.)

"I believe this nation should commit itself to achieving the goal, before this decade is out, of landing a man on the moon and returning him safely to the Earth." John F. Kennedy May 25, 1961

Borders and Lines

Objectives:

- Changing fonts and colors
- Drawing lines
- Changing width of lines
- Indenting text to wrap around pictures
- Resizing pictures
- Perfecting typing skills
- Adding borders

Application Needed:

Use an application in which you are able to add text, change color, add borders, draw lines, change thickness of lines, and add clip art.

Instructions:

1. Students should write original math word problems. For older students, story problems should be reasonably complex and require more than one step. You may suggest to younger students that they first write the problem on a piece of scrap paper.
2. Type the word problem.
3. Make sure the last line ends with a question and a question mark.
4. Draw a line for the answer. Thicken that line.
5. Add a border and suitable clip art.
6. Have students' double-check their problems before printing to find any errors.

Extension Ideas:

Use ideas that tie in with your curriculum. If you are studying the human body, have students write story problems that pertain to the body. For example, William's heart beats 70 times per minute. How many times does William's heart beat in 1 hour?

Another way that you could use this idea is for your morning exercises. Each day a different student could share his or her story problem for the entire class to solve. All of these math problems would make an attractive class bulletin board or a hall bulletin board where other classrooms could solve the problems, too.

Borders and Lines *(cont.)*

There are 20 homeroom classes at Indian River Junior High and 25 students in each homeroom. If 4 students from each homeroom class are using the Internet, how many total students are using the Internet?

Answer: _____

Attractive Advertisements

Objectives:

- Creating an attractive advertisement
- Enlarging font size
- Changing font style and color
- Accessing pictures from a CD-ROM
- Understanding correct proportions for a document

Application Needed:

Use a drawing application that is flexible but also can make professional-looking documents such as *Microsoft Publisher®* or applications in *Adobe Creative Suite®*.

Instructions:

1. Students will be creating advertisements for a particular event at school, such as a musical or a food drive. Assign students a topic and provide for them the who, what, where, and when facts.

2. Show students effective advertisements in a newspaper and compare those with poor advertisements.

3. Students will then construct their slogans or advertisements, remembering to include the important details. (Words should be highly visible and easy to read.)

4. Students may want to add a border or create their own.

5. Students should add appropriate clip art.

6. Finally, have them proof their work and print.

Extension Ideas:

A teacher could run a contest for the best advertisement, which would be voted on by students or faculty members. Also, a teacher could post a list of posters or advertisements that need to be made for other teachers or the administration. Students could earn community service hours upon completion of a project. Students could also create posters depicting the main characters from a novel read in class.

Attractive Advertisements *(cont.)*

Timelines

Objectives:

- Drawing boxes and lines
- Organizing data chronologically
- Inserting appropriate clip art
- Adjusting size of font and pictures to fit a page accordingly

Application Needed:

Students will need to use an application in which they can draw boxes, lines, and type information. Clip art will also be needed.

Instructions:

1. Have students list 8–10 main events in their lives, including birth.
2. Students will then draw the main bar for the timeline.
3. Draw a line going perpendicular from the main bar. Add a label to this line to represent the first item on the timeline (birth).
4. Have students continue making lines and labels for all the main events in their lives.
5. Find appropriate clip art for the timelines. (This is an excellent time to teach students how to access pictures from a CD-ROM or the Internet.)
6. Students should resize the pictures and labels to fit the page appropriately.
7. Add a title to the timeline. Change the font style and size.
8. Proofread, spell check, and then print.

Extension Ideas:

Timelines are a good way to display information and events chronologically. For a social studies unit, students could do the events that led to a particular president being elected or a timeline on the last few days of John F. Kennedy's life. Science teachers could have students chart the life of a salmon on a timeline.

Students always enjoy learning about the faculty at their school. They could interview faculty members and chart their important events on timelines displayed for other students to see.

Timelines *(cont.)*

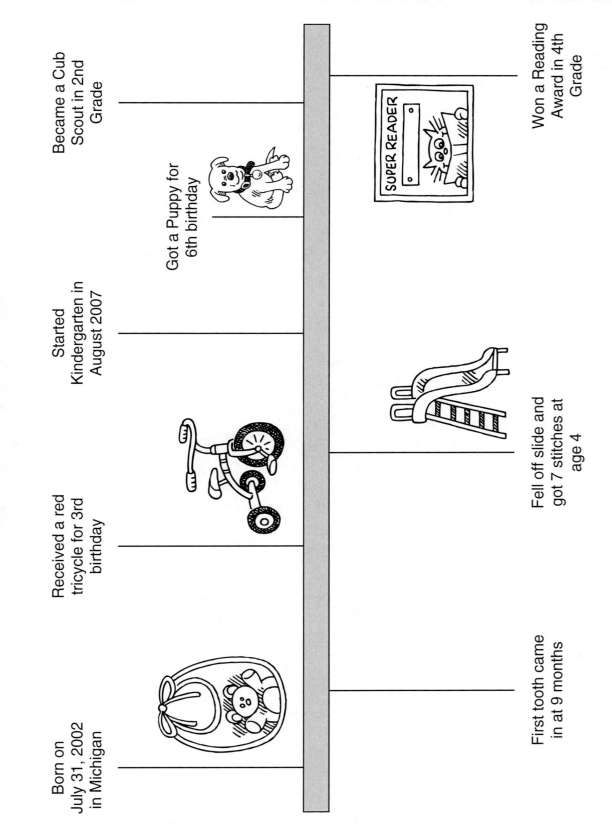

All About Me

Born on July 31, 2002 in Michigan

Received a red tricycle for 3rd birthday

Started Kindergarten in August 2007

Got a Puppy for 6th birthday

Became a Cub Scout in 2nd Grade

First tooth came in at 9 months

Fell off slide and got 7 stitches at age 4

SUPER READER

Won a Reading Award in 4th Grade

Making Projects Look Professional

Objectives:

- Making covers for projects
- Accessing clip art from CD-ROMS
- Accessing pictures from the Internet
- Enlarging font sizes
- Changing style of font

Application Needed:

Use an application such as *Microsoft Publisher*® that can easily be used to insert and move around clip art. Also, the application should allow you to type, enlarge, and change font.

Instructions:

1. Students will be creating covers for projects, such as a booklet on Washington, DC or a cover for an invention project.

2. Open the computer application selected for this project. Have students think about the general layout of their cover. Discuss layout options and give examples.

3. Have students type the title of their projects and their names. Student should enlarge the font considerably, probably to at least 60-point. Students may also highlight text and change the font if desired. Point out that writing should be larger than the pictures.

4. Let students use CD-ROMs and/or the Internet for appropriate pictures. Depending on the size of pictures and the amount of writing, students may want to use 4–6 pictures. Demonstrate how to copy and paste pictures from a CD-ROM and the Internet.

5. Finish the project cover, proof it, and print.

Extension Ideas:

Students can make covers for practically any project or book report. If students choose to do book-report covers, you may want them to draw one or two of the main characters by freehand and scan them onto the computer. Besides doing their project covers on the computer, students can do their entire projects as well.

ALL ABOUT
WASHINGTON, DC

The Food Guide

Objectives:

- Drawing a triangle
- Accessing specific pictures from a CD-ROM
- Adding text labels
- Researching on the Internet

Application Needed:

Use an application that the students can use to draw a large triangle, divide the triangle into sections, and paste pictures. Clip art will also be needed. Also if the teacher desires further food group research, the Internet should be accessible.

Instructions:

1. Students will need to become familiar with the food guide. (See the next page for an example.) Students will then be creating their own food guides with foods they like.
2. Draw an extra large triangle on the computer.
3. Divide the triangle up into appropriate food groups.
4. Have students label each section of the food guide and tell the number of servings suggested for each food group.
5. Supply students with clip-art pictures, perhaps from a CD-ROM, for their food guides. Students will choose foods that they like to fit into each category.
6. Work should be proofed and then printed.

Extension Ideas:

Teachers may want their students to do further research on the food guide. There are many food websites, including the following:

http://www.teachercreated.com/url-updates/2448-2. Click on page 136, site 1.

Students may want to write personal menus for one day that incorporate the correct servings suggested by the food guide. In addition, teachers may ask students to write everything they ate or drank in one day and compare their servings with the food guide's suggested servings.

The Food Guide (cont.)

My Food Guide

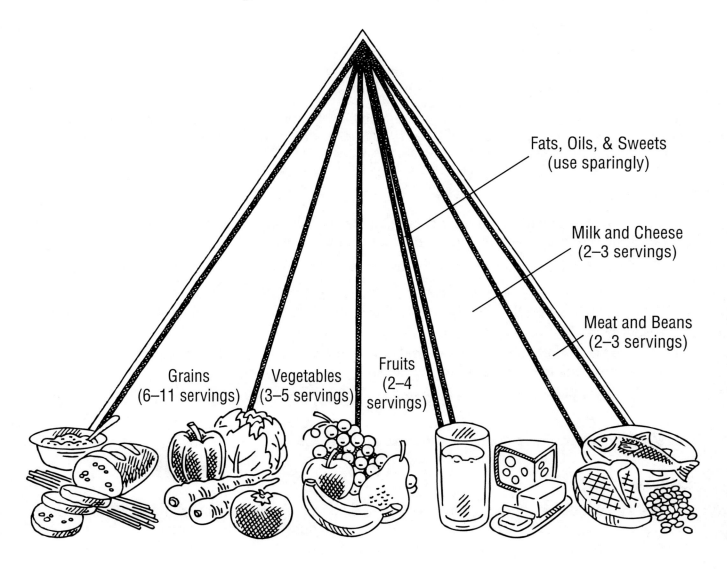

Fats, Oils, & Sweets
(use sparingly)

Milk and Cheese
(2–3 servings)

Meat and Beans
(2–3 servings)

Grains
(6–11 servings)

Vegetables
(3–5 servings)

Fruits
(2–4
servings)

Creating a Cookbook

Objectives:

- Understanding the basic format of a cookbook
- Writing fractions on the computer
- Making two columns of ingredients
- Spell-checking documents

Application Needed:

Use an application that not only word processes but also has flexibility to move things, enlarge fonts, and make columns. *Microsoft Word*® or *Microsoft PowerPoint*® will work well for this project.

Instructions:

1. Give the students a theme for this cookbook. It could tie in with a country the students are studying, such as a Spanish Cookbook or French Cookbook.

2. Students will then either create their own recipes or find one at home.

3. Students will then type their recipes. Give students exact specifications for typing their recipes, such as center title, font size of title should be 20 point, the recipe must fit on one page, etc.

4. Suggest that students put their ingredients into two columns if they have several items. Show students how to make two columns.

5. Once students have typed all of their information, they may need to enlarge or shrink the font to fill a page comfortably.

6. Work should be proofed, spell-checked, and then printed.

Extension Ideas:

Creating a cookbook is a great culminating project to many areas of study. In addition, students may want to make a school cookbook, having parents submit various recipes. Students could then sell these cookbooks to raise money for a particular sport or musical.

Creating a Cookbook (cont.)

Sour Cream Chocolate Cake

Ingredients:

2 cups (475 mL) flour

2 cups (475 mL) sugar

¾ cup (180 mL) sour cream

½ cup (120 mL) shortening

1 cup (240 mL) water

1 teaspoon (5 mL) baking soda

1 teaspoon (5mL) salt

1 teaspoon (5 mL) vanilla

½ teaspoon (2.5 mL) baking powder

2 eggs

4 squares unsweetened chocolate, melted and cooled

Heat oven to 350°F (180°C). Grease and flour two round pans. Beat all ingredients on low speed, scraping bowl constantly, for 30 seconds. Beat on high speed, scraping bowl occasionally, for 3 minutes. Pour into round pans.

Bake between 30–35 minutes until a wooden toothpick inserted in center comes out clean. Frost if desired.

Making a Menu

Objectives:

- Creating a menu for a restaurant
- Accessing pictures from the Internet
- Making many text frames and writing in them
- Exploring creativity through computer use
- Enlarging pictures and fonts to fill a page appropriately

Application Needed:

Use an application that not only word processes, but also has the flexibility to move objects, enlarge fonts, and add pictures. Clip art will also be needed. *Microsoft PowerPoint®* will work well for this project.

Instructions:

1. Each student will choose a theme for his or her menu, such as an African safari, dinosaurs, or French cuisine. Students may want to decide their theme based on the type of clip art that is available.

2. Students will then copy and paste five or six pictures from a CD-ROM or the Internet. Students should arrange the pictures throughout the menu.

3. Students should think of catchy titles for their menus.

4. Students will create menu items that correspond to their themes and pictures and change the font style and size to enhance the menu.

5. Once students have typed all of their information, they may need to enlarge or shrink the font to fill a page comfortably. Students should move the pictures around and resize them to fill the page.

6. Work should be proofed, spell-checked, and then printed.

Extension Ideas:

Creating menus is a fun way for students to express their creativity on the computer. The teacher may decide that creating a menu could be one assignment in a whole unit of study on a particular topic, such as Native Americans. Students could also create math problems that relate to their menus, such as "How many Elephant Dogs can Henry buy with $15.00?" Students may also want to help their school cafeteria by creating custom menus for each week or month.

Making a Menu (cont.)

Safari Inn

*

CHEESY LION'S PAW

$1.99

GRILLED CHEESE SERVED WITH
PICKLES ON THE SIDE

*

TIGER FRIES

$1.19

BIG SERVING OF FRIES
WITH MELTED CHEESE

DOUBLE-STACKED ZEBRA MELT

$3.79

TWO HAMBURGER PATTIES
PILED HIGH WITH CHEESE
ON A BUN

*

ELEPHANT DOG

$2.99

JUICY, FOOTLONG HOT DOG WITH
ALL OF THE FIXINGS

*

GIANT GIRAFFE

$1.29
EXTRA TALL
VANILLA SHAKE
WITH
SPRINKLES ON
TOP

Making a Menu (cont.)

Date: _____   Name: _____

Math Extensions for the Safari Inn Menu

Using the Safari Inn Menu, complete the questions below.

1. Karen wants to buy one Double-Stacked Zebra Melt, one Giant Giraffe, and one order of Tiger Fries. What will be Karen's total bill? _____

    How much change will Karen get back from a ten-dollar bill? _____

2. Which is more expensive, two Elephant Dogs or three Cheesy Lion's Paws? _____

    By how much? _____

3. For one week, Safari Inn counted how many Double Stacked Zebra Melts they sold. Monday—7, Tuesday—11, Wednesday—8, Thursday—5, Friday—14, Saturday—16, and Sunday—9. What was the average number of Zebra Melts the Safari Inn sold each day during this particular week? _____

4. Mr. Jones is having a birthday party for his son at the Safari Inn. Each person, including Mr. Jones, is having an Elephant Dog, a Giant Giraffe, and Tiger Fries.

    If there will be eight people at the party, how much will the total bill cost?

    _____

Appendix

Software Descriptions

Several types of software are used as the basis for the lessons in this book. The following descriptions explain the basic functions of each type of software and give examples. These definitions do not explain how specific software operates or provide ordering information on a particular package. These days it is common for there to be one or more free versions of each type of software, which can be found online by doing an Internet search.

Paint and Draw Software

Paint and draw software enables the user to create drawings and paintings on the computer. Many of the paint and draw tools mimic their physical counterparts such as the pencil tool or freeform tool that allows you to draw lines as you would with a pencil; the paintbrush tool, which is similar to a paintbrush; and the stamp function, which is like a rubber stamp. The paint and draw software, however, has additional tools that are not available elsewhere. For example, the straight-line tool draws a straight line; the shape tools create a particular shape in different sizes, and the flood fill (paint bucket) fills in a shape completely with a designated color or pattern.

Paint files can be saved or printed just as text files are. Clip art can be created in paint software and used in other applications such as multimedia slide shows or stories that have been word processed.

There are many different software packages on the market, some more complex than others. Be sure to use a paint and draw application appropriate for students' skills and abilities.

Spreadsheet Software

Spreadsheet software enables the user to enter numbers and formulas into a grid or chart-style format. Formulas automatically perform the calculation on the entered numbers. This provides the user with answers quickly and accurately. Many spreadsheet applications also have a graphing function that works with a spreadsheet to create graphic representations of data.

Graphing Software

Graphing software is often included in other types of software such as word-processing applications, spreadsheet applications, or suites. The graphing software utilizes the entered numbers or data to create graphical representations of the data in various forms. Most graphing software can create professional looking bar charts, pie charts, and scatter and bubble charts. Colors can be added to make the charts easy to read.

Database Software

Database software enables the user to enter data collected on a particular topic into a file that has been formatted in a particular way. Fields or categories of data within the topic must be selected and entered into the database file. Data is entered into each field and then saved to create a record within the database. A collection of records is a file. When the database is complete, information about the data can be obtained by having the computer search the database or sort the files looking for specific information. The database user can enter questions formatted in a particular way to access information in the database. The user should consult the instruction manual to learn the format for queries.

Spreadsheet software that is compatible with a database package can have cells that access certain fields in the database files and automatically update the figures in the fields as they are changed in the database. The spreadsheet then automatically performs required calculations on the new figures.

Multimedia Authoring Software

This type of software is called authoring software because it allows the user to create or author a package. Multimedia refers to combining different types of media or communication such as text, sound, animation, video, and graphics. Most of these packages use the card or slide-show format. The user creates cards or slides that are connected together.

There are mainly two types of multimedia authoring software: linear and nonlinear. Linear automatically connects slides to each other in the order in which they were created. When the slide is completed, the user clicks on the mouse to move to the next slide. Slides cannot be taken out of order but they can be skipped or hidden in most packages. Earlier versions of this type of software did not always allow sound or animation to be included, but newer versions have these features.

Nonlinear authoring software allows the user to move through slides in any order or move back to slides already shown through the creation of hyper buttons or hot buttons. These buttons generally are multifunctional and allow the user to choose the function of the button, including which slide to go to next. This type of multimedia software is newer and usually allows the user more flexibility of use. Graphics and sound brought in from various sources can be added to the slides, along with animation and videos.

Word-Processing Software

Word-processing software enables the user to enter text by typing on the keyboard. The entered text can be easily changed and edited. Most word-processing applications offer a spell-check feature that automatically searches out the misspelled words and typos and assists with corrections. Many word-processing applications also offer a grammar-check feature that checks sentence structure, word usage, and punctuation.

Suites

Suites are software packages that combine some of the above listed software applications. These packages provide the user with word-processing, spreadsheet, database, and graphing software that is compatible and easy to use. Users can move data between the various applications. For example, information entered in a database can also be entered as a text document in a word-processing application. Spreadsheets can automatically access the data entered in a database and perform the required calculations.